Every day, the news highlights challenges in workplace culture and gender pay gaps. Roxanne's book confronts these issues with courage and clarity. Drawing from her own experiences and those of other experts, Roxanne offers invaluable insights and practical tips through powerful storytelling. This compelling book reminds readers that they are not alone on their journey. It provides a toolkit for building resilience, reassuring us that we can achieve success without changing who we are.

—**Dr Sue Slowikowski,** Charles Sturt University

You're holding in your hand a promise. A promise of inspiration and insight, and Roxanne Calder keeps her promises. She is passionate about furthering women's careers, a gifted recruiter and a dedicated professional who looks past the CV to the person and their dreams.

—**Heather Swan,** World Record Holding Wingsuit Pilot

Roxanne doesn't just have her finger on the pulse of Aussie workplaces! She knows what's actually happening in them and how work is changing. Her insights are razor sharp, informative and important.

—**Mary Madigan,** writer and journalist

I have worked with Roxanne Calder for over a decade and it has always been a pleasure. She is across both the big picture and the little details that make a difference and her advice is always insightful. Rox's books are a testament to her knowledge and her generosity, designed to enrich opportunities for others. I always come away from our meetings refreshed and feeling inspired.

—**Dijanna Mulhearn,** author, presenter and doctoral researcher

EARNING POWER

EARNING POWER

Breaking Barriers and Building Wealth for Women

ROXANNE CALDER

WILEY

First published 2025 by John Wiley & Sons Australia, Ltd

© John Wiley & Sons Australia, Ltd 2025

All rights reserved, including rights for text and data mining and training of artificial intelligence technologies or similar technologies. Except as permitted under the *Australian Copyright Act 1968* (for example, a fair dealing for the purposes of study, research, criticism or review) no part of this publication may be reproduced, stored in a retrieval system, or transmitted, in any form or by any means, electronic, mechanical, photocopying, recording or otherwise. Advice on how to obtain permission to reuse material from this title is available at http://www.wiley.com/go/permissions.

The right of Roxanne Calder to be identified as the author of *Earning Power* has been asserted in accordance with law.

ISBN: 978-1-394-31343-3

A catalogue record for this book is available from the National Library of Australia

Registered Office
John Wiley & Sons Australia, Ltd. Level 4, 600 Bourke Street, Melbourne, VIC 3000, Australia

For details of our global editorial offices, customer services, and more information about Wiley products visit us at www.wiley.com.

Wiley also publishes its books in a variety of electronic formats and by print-on-demand. Some content that appears in standard print versions of this book may not be available in other formats.

Trademarks: Wiley and the Wiley logo are trademarks or registered trademarks of John Wiley & Sons, Inc. and/or its affiliates in the United States and other countries and may not be used without written permission. All other trademarks are the property of their respective owners. John Wiley & Sons, Inc. is not associated with any product or vendor mentioned in this book.

Limit of Liability/Disclaimer of Warranty
While the publisher and author have used their best efforts in preparing this work, they make no representations or warranties with respect to the accuracy or completeness of the contents of this work and specifically disclaim all warranties, including without limitation any implied warranties of merchantability or fitness for a particular purpose. No warranty may be created or extended by sales representatives, written sales materials or promotional statements for this work. This work is sold with the understanding that the publisher is not engaged in rendering professional services. The advice and strategies contained herein may not be suitable for your situation. You should consult with a specialist where appropriate. The fact that an organisation, website, or product is referred to in this work as a citation and/or potential source of further information does not mean that the publisher and author endorse the information or services the organisation, website, or product may provide or recommendations it may make. Further, readers should be aware that websites listed in this work may have changed or disappeared between when this work was written and when it is read. Neither the publisher nor author shall be liable for any loss of profit or any other commercial damages, including but not limited to special, incidental, consequential, or other damages.

Cover design by Wiley
Photo of Nagi Maehashi (p.xvii): Rob Palmer
Photo of Professor Fiona Wood AO (p.xviii): Marnie Richardson Photography
Figure 6.1 (tree): © great_kit / Adobe Stock; © mithun1990 / Adobe Stock

Set in 12/14pt BemboStd by Straive, Chennai, India

SKY6CB0B85F-F330-4BF7-B478-ACC953B9205D_022025

*I dedicate this book to my family, my patient and caring partner,
Richard, my dad, mum, sister and brother,
BFF Daisy and beautiful Lily.*

CONTENTS

Introduction: Who wears the pants?		*xi*
Contributors		*xvii*
1	Gender bias in days gone by	1
2	Gender bias today: still alive and well	19
3	Female worth: the reality of the gender pay gap	35
4	What could you do with $1 million?	49
5	The million-dollar formula	77
6	False beliefs and traps	105
7	What he said: insights and advice for men	127
8	Harnessing your support network	145
9	Tools and tips from dream achievers	167
Conclusion: I fought a boy and won		*187*
Notes		*193*

Introduction

WHO WEARS THE PANTS?

In 1995, gender equality was a distant dream. For starters, where I worked, the company policy for women was 'skirts only'. Matching suit jackets were, of course, also the norm. Trousers were not allowed, and stockings or pantyhose were a must. No bare legs, no open-toed or flat shoes and categorically no trainers. The word used in the policy manual was 'polished'. As for 'casual Fridays', we didn't have them. There was no negotiation, compromise or pandering. If you didn't like it, you didn't join the company

The economic conditions were also vastly different. When I entered the workforce—with youth unemployment at 28.1 per cent and the overall unemployment rate at 10 per cent—I was grateful to have any job. With the surplus of job seekers, there was always someone ready and available to take your position. Being so easily replaceable was part of the psychological carry-all you took with you to work.

Just before starting my new job, I was to learn the gravity of the 'no pants' policy. I nervously but oh so carefully selected an outfit to wear when returning my signed contract. It was a cool August day and I remember wearing navy woollen tailored Country Road pants, a fitted, grey, long-sleeved cotton top, also from Country Road, and brown Timberland loafers. It was the quintessential 1990s preppy look and I had it down pat!

My boss, however, was not impressed. She took my contract, shook my hand and with an assertive, throaty laugh, said, 'You won't be wearing that outfit on Monday.' It was the pants. I'm tough-skinned, but I was taken aback. I had always been, and remain, a tiny bit rebellious—not to mention an enormous and sometimes annoying supporter of female 'anything'. I loved being a 'girl' but pushed the boundaries on how that was defined, especially when it came to competing with males.

As a child, I was described as 'complex', and I'm certain my parents were frequently confounded. I was the tomboy building rafts, but I had a Barbie, a doll's house and every other doll imaginable. I wore surfer-style boys' board shorts but, at the same time, insisted on the fashionable 1970s maxi dresses, long boots and Farrah Fawcett (*Charlie's Angels*) hairstyle. I challenged the boys at school, never tolerated their nonsense and aspired to have a 'man's job' when I grew up. I wanted to be an engineer, like my dad—that is, until I realised it involved physics.

So, the 'no pants' policy was confronting and a tough pill to swallow. But I am a huge pragmatist and a bit vain. Frankly, I don't look great in trousers. My legs aren't long enough to carry the look. The Country Road ones were pretty much my limit and only on 'skinny days'. I tackled the dilemma in the practical way I usually do: I preferred skirts anyway, so I got on with it.

I should mention I was also conditioned. In a world where conformity often disguised itself as tradition, I was conditioned to accept a 'no trouser policy' as perfectly acceptable. I mean, my own school, which I had left not that long before, had a skirts-only rule. I was also conditioned to accept and not question authority (another sign of the times). Despite my innate rebellious disposition, I accept authority when I respect it, and I respected and trusted my new bosses. I was hungry to embark on my career and to learn all I could.

It might seem disappointing to contemporary readers that my boss—being a woman—enforced a 'skirts only' policy. Don't be too quick to judge though. It was a necessary and clever approach to navigating the bias and discrimination of the 1990s, which was rife. The aim of the policy was for women to 'fit in'. My boss was a feminist, and her goal was to empower other women. She also innately and intuitively understood that women needed to fit in by stealth back then.

By 'fitting in' when we went to a meeting—which was typically run by a male 20 years older than us—we lessoned the likelihood of judgement and rejection. I assure you, if I went to a meeting back then in jeans or looking remotely masculine in trousers—or didn't wear a jacket or heels, for that matter—it is safe to say the client would have chosen another consultant to work with. Someone 'more professional'.

I am grateful to have worked in such a culture in my formative years. Being a pragmatist, the emphasis on presentation and business polish at that age helped me to overcome feelings of self doubt and instead instilled in me confidence and pride. I felt empowered despite, or maybe because of, the mandated skirt culture. My strong value set and ardent belief in supporting all things female remain, and have developed into a job with purpose in a profession I love.

I have the fondest memories of my first 'proper' job due to the amazing and powerful women I worked with. They were innovative, entrepreneurial and pushed all boundaries. I was given every opportunity to shine and advance, and I took it. When I interview women today, they often tell me they don't want to work for a female boss or in a predominantly female environment. I am perplexed and saddened when I hear this and think, 'Oh, shame, you don't know what you are missing out on!'

Today I run my own recruitment business, EST10. I have managed corporate recruitment firms throughout Australia, the UK, Singapore and Hong Kong. I have completed my MBA, and *Earning Power* is my second book. I know the workplace back to front: I have placed thousands of women in jobs and assisted thousands more with career advice.

The attitudes of 1995 are thankfully in the past. The 'skirts only' policies are long gone. But don't be fooled: the sayonara is superficial. I consider it a token gesture by society and corporations. I am sure it's only intended to keep us quiet for a bit. A stall tactic even. But not if, like me, you stand up for those who can't, and choke loudly on injustice.

So what is the real litmus test for gender equality? The ultimate truth serum? It's pay equity. Progress in this area is practically prehistoric. In March 2023, the Australian federal parliament passed the *Workplace Gender Equality Amendment (Closing the Gender Pay Gap) Bill 2023*.

Ahem ... that's nearly 30 years after our 'skirts only' era, and the only way to achieve pay equity is by enshrining it in law. A stark reality, difficult to comprehend and even harder to accept in our supposedly enlightened times.

As a recruitment expert who has worked with countless women over the years, I can attest to the harsh reality of the earnings discrepancies. The inequities are bold, in your face and, sadly, entrenched—and the facts back this up.

$1 million and counting...

Data and statistics show women to be consistently financially worse off than men. The average gender-based pay discrepancy over a lifetime is $1 million ... and counting. Along comes retirement, and it's too late.

I've long known about the million-dollar disparity in earnings. I formulated my own calculations and estimates long ago, and I am not sure whether to be deeply concerned or somewhat proud that my findings are eerily similar to those of the Workplace Gender Equality Agency (WGEA).

Financial independence empowers and liberates. Financial resources grant us the freedom to choose our own paths in life, fostering responsibility, innovation and creativity. What I cherish most about economic independence is the ability to help others. So yes, while women benefit from financial independence, so does society.

The workplace gender law underscores the harsh reality of wage inequality. It rightfully points the finger at companies, executives and society. The WGEA, and others, attribute the gap in earnings to social, economic and structural factors. They are accurate in their assessments and the external pressure is necessary and justified.

Still, it's not enough. Waiting for these structural changes to 'make things better', fair and equitable is simply too long. At this pace, even our grandchildren will be too old to benefit from the reforms.

When it comes to my future, I have a problem attributing accountability and responsibility solely to external forces. And it's not a debate on whether what they are saying is right or wrong. It's more about it being out of my control and in the hands of others.

I've never been good at handing over control, especially when it has to do with my earnings, finances, dreams and future. This might be why I am often considered pushy, ballsy or bossy. This also might be why this rebellious 'pro-female anything' advocate has written this book.

The premise of *Earning Power* is self-efficacy: to help women be in control of their financial future, to earn more and work towards closing the gender pay gap for themselves. It looks at the gender pay gap from a different angle — an employment and personal agency lens — and distils my experience and knowledge to help women to be a million dollars ahead in life.

My expertise is recruitment, career advice and the employment arena. It has been my playground for more than 30 years. I know the swings that give you reach, the slides too precarious to even try and the monkey bars to risk a thrill on. Mostly, I know the players, bullies, imposters, victims, tricksters, saboteurs, cheerleaders, mentors, givers, takers and more.

The data and case studies I present hone in on the impact of gender bias and discrimination on maintaining pay inequity. In case you're wondering, their contribution is hefty.

Discrimination and bias range from the obvious (such as blatant sexism) to the subtle, ingrained beliefs that hold women back. Gender bias accounts for the assumptions and decisions others make that leave women a million dollars behind in lifetime earnings. As for the subtle, ingrained beliefs? These are the ones that sneak in and become part of our self-concept: hesitating to put our hand up, downplaying achievements, underestimating and undermining ourselves ... and the list continues. They may be subtle, but they pack a big punch.

The effect of the daily burden of bias and discrimination cannot be overstated. It is chronic, takes its toll and accumulates. The worst part is most of us don't even know we are affected.

Earning Power holds to account the external structural factors that see women in a position of entrenched financial disadvantage. However, I should point out that my expertise is not in policy. I don't attempt to provide solutions to the structural barriers. I see them and know only too well they exist. Therefore, I am grateful to people who take this up as their cause: people such as Future Women's Helen McCabe and Jamila Rizvi, along with countless other brave and compassionate individuals.

There are several pivotal points in our working lives; crucial decisions that can shape how the rest of our lives may fall. In this book, I specifically explore the workplace decisions: small, incremental, yet brave and meaningful decisions women make that might seem trivial at the time but carry profound ramifications and consequences. By raising awareness of these critical junctures, we can dramatically alter life's outcomes in a big way, to the effect of $1 million.

This is not a career guidance book. Nor am I suggesting you need a career to have financial security and independence. You don't. However, I am advocating that women can do more for themselves and take the million-dollar earnings discrepancy into their own hands to effect change.

Walk with me through these pages and see how small changes to your mindset and decisions can empower you to earn your worth. I hope it equates to a million dollars and more over your lifetime.

CONTRIBUTORS

In writing this book, I had the privilege of seeking counsel from six remarkable women and one distinguished man. It has been an honour to learn from their insights and hear their stories, and I am deeply grateful for the time they so generously shared with me.

Julia Ross

EX GLOBAL CEO, ROSS HUMAN DIRECTIONS

Following a successful career in the UK, culminating in Julia being a finalist for the Veuve Clicquot 'Woman of the Year' award at age 22, Julia moved to Australia. There she spearheaded the expansion of an international HR group, opening branches throughout Australia, New Zealand and Asia.

In Sydney, Julia's entrepreneurial spirit led her to start Julia Ross Recruitment. Using leading-edge industry unique and pioneering service offerings, the group quickly became one of Australia's fastest-growing companies. Listing the company on the Australian Stock Exchange (ASX) as Ross Human Directions, Julia continued to break barriers and became the first, and only ever, female owner of a company to do so.

Julia is well known for her philanthropy and community contributions. Notably, Julia had the honour of delivering the welcome speech for President Clinton during his Australian tour, helping to increase the profile of and secure crucial funds for the Sydney Children's Hospital.

Being an early adopter and part of the new breed of socially conscious entrepreneurs, Julia prioritised society's wellbeing ahead of pure financial gain. Today, Julia serves as an angel investor for a number of female-led start-ups, and gives her experience and knowledge to foster their success. Julia holds steadfast to her core ethos of 'creating strong communities and sustainability over gain'.

Peta Credlin AO

POLITICAL ANALYST

Peta Credlin AO is a political analyst who hosts her top-rating prime time programme *Credlin* on Sky News and is a national columnist with both *The Australian* and News Corp Sunday newspapers (*The Sunday Telegraph, Sunday Herald-Sun* and Queensland's *Sunday Mail*). She is a law graduate of the University of Melbourne and has post-graduate qualifications from the ANU. For some time she has been involved with the University of Melbourne's School of Government as an Honorary Professorial Fellow and several not-for-profit boards.

For 16 years, Peta was a senior ministerial adviser in the Howard Government. Between 2009 and 2015, she was Chief of Staff to the Hon Tony Abbott AC during his time as Leader of the Opposition and later as Prime Minister of Australia. She is one of the longest serving chiefs of staff to a political leader. In the 2021 Queen's Birthday Honours, Peta Credlin was appointed an Officer of the Order of Australia for 'distinguished service to parliament and politics, to policy development, and to the executive function of government'.

Peta is admitted as a Barrister and Solicitor in Victoria. In 2015, she received the Australian Women's Leadership Award (ACT) and was named a joint winner of Harper Bazaar's 'Woman of the Year' (2016). She is a joint Walkley Award winner (2016) and TV Week Logie Award winner (2017) for her role in Sky News Australia's 2016 Federal Election coverage. In 2021, Peta won a Kennedy Award for 'Excellence in Journalism' and in 2021 and 2024, a News Award for 'Achievements in Specialist Journalism'.

Nagi Maehashi

FOUNDER, RECIPETIN EATS

Nagi Maehashi is the voice, cook, photographer and videographer behind the phenomenally popular recipe site RecipeTin Eats. A former finance executive, Nagi started RecipeTin Eats in 2014 to share her passion for creating affordable everyday meals with the 'wow' factor and classic dishes of the world done right. She has a devoted worldwide following with billions of views of her website and an extraordinary social media following. In 2021, Nagi founded her food bank, RecipeTin Meals, which cooks and donates 130 000 meals (including desserts) annually to those in need and the vulnerable.

Nagi's first cookbook, *Dinner* — launched in 2022 — is the fastest-selling cookbook in Australian publishing history.

In 2023, it became the first cookbook to win the Australian Book Industry Award's Book of the Year. Following on from *Dinner*, Nagi has recently launched her second cookbook, *Tonight*, solving the perennial problem of 'What's for dinner tonight?'

Nagi lives on the northern beaches of Sydney with her golden retriever, Dozer, Australia's favourite taste tester.

Professor Fiona Wood AO

FRCS, FRACS, PLASTIC RECONSTRUCTIVE SURGEON AND WORLD-LEADING BURNS SPECIALIST

Professor Fiona Wood has been a burns surgeon and researcher for more than 30 years and is director of the Burns Service of Western Australia (BSWA). She is a consultant plastic surgeon at Fiona Stanley Hospital and the Perth Children's Hospital; co-founder of the first skin cell laboratory in Western Australia; Winthrop Professor in the School of Surgery at The University of Western Australia; and co-founder of the Fiona Wood Foundation (formerly The McComb Foundation). She is also the leading Australian plastic surgeon and the co-inventor of ReCell, a spray-on skin technique for burn victims.

Fiona's greatest contribution and enduring legacy is her work with co-inventor Marie Stoner, pioneering the innovative 'spray-on skin' technique (ReCell), which is today used worldwide.

In October 2002, Fiona was propelled into the media spotlight when most of the survivors from the Bali bombings arrived in Perth, where Fiona led the medical team at Royal Perth Hospital to save many lives.

Throughout Fiona's career, she has received prestigious accolades in recognition of her clinical excellence and burns research outputs, which have improved the quality-of-life outcomes of burn patients locally and worldwide.

Kristina Karlsson

FOUNDER, KIKKI.K

Swedish-born Kristina was the founder of kikki.K and, more recently, Dream Life (an inspiring and empowering brand-turned-global movement). After growing up on a small farm in Sweden, at the age of 22 she found herself in Australia, half a world away from family and friends, with little money.

Kristina sold all she owned to create and build globally loved Swedish design and stationery business kikki.K from the ground up, opening 120 award-winning retail stores in five countries with a passionate team of approximately 1500. The online store served stationery and design lovers in over 150 countries, achieving a total revenue of around $650 million.

For more than 20 years, Kristina won the hearts and minds of millions the world over as the creative force and personality behind what was a purpose-led brand. After a tumultuous experience through the COVID pandemic forced the closure of her stores, Kristina lost control of kikki.K and parted ways with the company in heart-breaking circumstances.

She has since bounced back and is on a mission to inspire and empower 101 million people the world over to discover and chase their dreams.

Leila McKinnon

JOURNALIST AND TELEVISION PRESENTER

Leila McKinnon is a versatile broadcaster, narrator, writer and reporter with a career that began as a cadet in Rockhampton, where she covered everything from cattle to courts. She quickly made her mark at the Nine Network, reporting and presenting for *Nine Gold Coast News* before moving to Brisbane to join *A Current Affair*.

In 2001, Leila moved to Sydney as a news reporter and subsequently became newsreader for the *Today* show. Her role expanded further when she became Nine's North American correspondent in Los Angeles, covering major stories across the United States and co-hosting the network's health series *What's Good For You*.

Leila has interviewed seven Australian Prime Ministers (and Beyoncé — twice!) and regularly hosts *A Current Affair* and *Today*. She's also led coverage for major events such as the State of Origin, the Commonwealth Games, the London Olympics and, most recently, the Paris 2024 Olympics. Beyond television, Leila is a book reviewer and podcaster, and she serves on the board of the Ricky Stuart Foundation, which builds hospice centres for children and adults with autism.

Philip Kearns AM

EX WALLABIES RUGBY UNION CAPTAIN AND CEO OF AV JENNINGS

Phil Kearns, one of rugby's most famous and respected sons, is also a successful businessman, sports commentator, family man and charity worker. Acknowledged by many rugby commentators as having been the world's best rugby hooker, Phil debuted in 1989 and played 67 test matches for Australia, captaining 10. Phil is one of only 43 players who have won multiple Rugby World Cups, and capped his rugby career as part of the Wallabies' World Cup win in 1999, his third World Cup campaign. Since 2022 Phil has been CEO of AV Jennings, one of Australia's most recognised leading residential property development companies.

Outside of work, Phil is an avid family man with four children. He also maintains commitments with numerous charities and not-for-profits, including establishing the Balmoral Burn, an annual charity run up one of Sydney's steepest streets that raises funds for children's services—which he organised with the Humpty Dumpty Foundation—and as an ambassador for the Minerva Network. To top it off, Phil has raced the Sydney to Hobart Yacht Race three times. Phil was appointed a Member of the Order of Australia in 2017 for significant service to the community through support for charitable organisations, business and rugby union at the elite level. He was also inducted into the Australian Rugby Hall of Fame in 2018 and the NSW Rugby Hall of Fame in 2024.

Chapter 1

GENDER BIAS IN DAYS GONE BY

Mistaking the female boss walking into the boardroom for an assistant. Saying women are too emotional or 'soft' to be good leaders. Overlooking a woman for a promotion because she's just back from maternity leave and you assume the extra responsibility will be 'too much'. Saying 'he' when describing an accountant, doctor, pilot or any authority figure.

All the above are examples of the gender biases happening every day that impact women's careers.

Embarrassingly, I did this very thing when drafting chapter 4 of this book. I referred to the accountant as 'he'! When I realised what I'd done, I shrank in mortified shame and slowly peered around my desk. *Did anyone see?* I found myself wanting to believe that my preference for a male accountant was just a coincidence. However, I have to confess, there was bias at play.

If you find yourself in a similar situation, it is good to remember that we all have some form of bias, and it doesn't mean we are bad human beings. However, we should be aware of our biases and inclinations and question the basis of our beliefs and assumptions. They form the foundation of how we act, behave and speak. If they aren't kept in check, they continue to recycle and perpetuate.

Biases can be conscious (explicit) or unconscious (implicit). An explicit bias is when you consciously hold stereotypical attitudes or beliefs about a person or group. An implicit bias is hidden and outside a person's consciousness. It is expressed automatically, without conscious awareness.

Implicit biases are subtle. They are the undercurrents of our minds, operating beneath the surface of conscious awareness. They are like shadows cast by the experiences and associations we've absorbed over time, influencing our actions without us realising it.

Imagine a hiring manager who genuinely believes in their commitment to diversity. Yet, when reviewing résumés, they unknowingly favour candidates with names that sound familiar or reflect their own cultural background. All the while, they remain blissfully unaware their decision-making is being subtly swayed by an unseen hand. This is the insidious nature of implicit bias: working silently and persistently, and often beyond our immediate comprehension, shaping our judgements in ways that seem entirely rational to us, even as they perpetuate the very disparities we claim to oppose.

The fact is we are all biased. Biases are an inescapable part of being human. Most biases we have learned are taught to us by our environment, culture, society, parents and school, to name a few. The reason bias persists is because it serves a cognitive purpose. We use bias as an efficiency measure, a shortcut to process information. Gordon Allport's book *The Nature of Prejudice* refers to bias as our 'very human tendency to classify people into categories in order to quickly process information and make sense of the world'. We have done this daily since we were children.

A research study from the University of British Columbia (UBC) showed that babies from the age of one demonstrate positive bias for speakers of their first language — that is, the language spoken by their primary caregivers.[1] The babies also expected the speakers to be prosocial, and when they witnessed antisocial behaviour, the babies showed surprise. The results of this study suggest that 'babies do not develop a negative bias towards cultures, people or sounds until later in childhood, making negative biases more likely to be learned behaviour than innate'.[2]

The findings of this research from UBC challenge the notion that negative biases are inherent, revealing they are shaped by the environments in which we develop. As children grow, they are influenced by the societal norms, cultural narratives and behaviours around them, which shape their perceptions and attitudes. Infants start life without these biases, highlighting the role of socialisation in their formation. Through exposure to external influences, media, education and interactions, children learn to categorise and judge. However, it's important to acknowledge that individual personality traits and neurodevelopment factors can also influence how children internalise these influences. This underscores the importance of fostering inclusive environments early on, as these experiences shape attitudes carried into adulthood.

The power of 'I can'

Julia Ross, Fiona Wood, Leila McKinnon, Kristina Karlsson, Peta Credlin and Nagi Maehashi all share one crucial trait: they never thought they 'couldn't'.

All of these remarkable women from different backgrounds and industries grew up with a strong belief in their own abilities. When I interviewed Julia and Fiona — who, incidentally, both grew up in the UK before coming to Australia — they spoke of their childhood as instrumental to their belief in self. As Fiona puts it, 'I was brought up with a solid belief you can do anything if you are prepared to work hard enough. And that is what I came to the table with: capacity.'

Julia talks about growing up with the early influence and belief that 'there wasn't anything I couldn't do. I had no perception or preconditioning that I wouldn't be able to do something and I took that with me to the corporate world. From a gender viewpoint, it's so important as many women are preconditioned to think a certain way.'

Kristina's tale is nearly identical. 'Growing up on a farm in Sweden, I never saw myself as different from a male.' Peta says, 'I want to write my own history' and from her early foundations, growing up in the country she was encouraged to 'speak up' and 'be heard.'

Leila and Nagi tell a similar story. Leila says, 'I always thought, well, if other people can do it, I can too.' Nagi says, 'Growing up and in my life, I have always been surrounded by strong women. I don't know any different.'

What is evident from their journeys is their determination and hard work. Leila talks of her first job as a journalist cadet and says, 'In the back of my mind, I thought, "I'm not going to fail. I'm going to work hard and do whatever I can". I've always been good at backing myself and being a little bit bullish.'

Nagi says of her first job, also a cadetship, 'I worked my guts out from day one.' Then, later, in forming RecipeTin Eats, 'I worked so hard and ridiculous hours and there were times when I broke down. But you just pick yourself up, dust yourself off and keep going.'

It was an inspiration and privilege to meet and interview these women. Growing up in an environment that fostered encouragement and instilled a strong belief in one's capabilities and potential—an environment that consistently said, 'you can'—speaks volumes about their achievements and the legacy they will leave.

It wasn't all rosy, though, and it wasn't a given. Their perseverance made the difference.

Bias and discrimination

Bias doesn't operate in a vacuum; it often finds its most damaging expression in the form of discrimination. Bias is an inclination or prejudice for or against something or someone, often subconscious, while discrimination is the treatment of individuals based on that bias. So, when we have gender bias, we favour one gender over another based on our preconceived notions about gender roles and identities. The problem, from what I can see, is that we tend to give more airplay and intrinsically higher value to masculine attributes and downplay the value of feminine ones.

What about the other biases such as race and ageism? Have you noticed that for these biases we are still comfortable calling someone out by labelling them racist or ageist? But when it comes to bias that is gender related, we don't as frequently see a firm and definite call out; discussions tend to focus on broader concepts, and the term 'sexism' is less commonly used.

Instead, we softened the language to 'gender bias'. I question the necessity of this euphemism when we know that 36 per cent of the gender pay gap stems directly from discrimination.[3] How can we close the earnings gap when we can't label the issue correctly?

Anything less feels like a cover-up, obscuring the truth with half-measures and perpetuating the inequities we aim to resolve. If we are to genuinely address and correct the inequity that women face, we must confront it with honesty and courage.

For the sake of formalities, let's look at the differences. Genderism (gender bias) — or bias resulting from a gender binary view — is a system of beliefs that perpetuates negative evaluations of gender nonconformity.[4] Sexism — defined as prejudice or discrimination based on one's sex — stems from an ideology that one sex is superior to the other.[5] A prejudice is an opinion or attitude about a group or individual, often rooted in ignorance, fear or deep-seated bias.

We live in a time where societal understanding of gender fluidity and individual identity is evolving at a rapid pace. This book analyses the traditional aspects of gender bias that continue to affect so many women. That said, women who are non–gender conforming—who are trans or from LGBTIQ+

communities — experience additional forms of discrimination. I'm not able to cover all forms of discrimination in this book. Still, I am mindful of the need for ongoing examination of the issues that all women face across the spectrum of identity.

Here are some stories of what gender bias — I mean sexism — looked like in days gone by. I must be honest: it doesn't feel like that long ago.

Honey, there's no milk in the fridge

It is 2001. My boss, Julia Ross, was CEO of the ASX-listed global company Ross Human Directions. The important detail about this story is that my CEO, as you may have picked up, was a 'she'. At this stage of my career, I had worked my way up and proudly held a senior role, reporting directly to Julia.

The story starts on a Friday morning. Twelve months earlier, Julia had listed Ross Human Directions on the ASX, through an IPO, for just over $57 million. At the time, it was the largest ever single-owner business and the only solely female-owned business to list on the ASX. Not only that, but I believe this was also a global record.

It was 7.45 am. We were always early starters, and as Julia was sipping her tea, taking her vitamins and simultaneously applying her mascara, she casually shared her tale. The previous night, as she arrived home and walked in the door after a long and hectic day, her long-term partner called out from in front of the TV, 'Honey, there's no milk in the fridge.' The unspoken message was, 'Before you sit down, you'd better quickly run out and buy some milk *because, after all, that's your job.*'

I shrank in my chair. Julia was as cool as ice and matter-of-fact. She turned to me, mascara wand in hand. With timing only professional comedians master and with her gifted, penetrating, green-eyed stare, shrug of her shoulders and palms facing up she said, 'Can you believe it, Rox? I mean, *can you believe it?*'

Her indignation was palpable. There was some frustration too, but mostly a resolute, deflated understanding that this was what she constantly dealt with. In today's talk, it would be 'WTF', but I've never heard or known Julia to swear.

Somehow, despite the extent of her responsibilities — 20 offices throughout Australia; seven more in London, Dublin, Hong Kong, Singapore and New Zealand; circa 500 employees; revenue of more than $350 million; unforgiving shareholders; a relentlessly demanding board; and being described by one analyst as 'probably the most aggressive, determined, tough chief executive I know' — it was also her job, that Thursday evening, to ensure there was milk in the fridge.

Back then, at the tender age of 33, I recall thinking, 'Oh, maybe you could have picked it up on the way home.' When I think of that today, I am embarrassed. I get it now. It wasn't about being grounded enough to do a grocery run — it was the blind disregard of the level of responsibility and laden load she was already carrying. This was gender bias loud and clear. No doubt it was not intentional — and that's what made it hurtful. No matter her achievements and workload, it seemed, her job was seen as a hobby, and nothing very serious: 'You're a female CEO — how cute'.

For more context, in 1995, 0 per cent of CEOs in Fortune 500 companies were women.[6] As at June 2023, a sparse 10.4 per cent of Fortune 500 companies were run by women and in one-quarter of these the leaders had become CEOs during the previous year.[7]

What's more, *Women's Agenda* reported that in 2023 only about 10.5 per cent of ASX 200 leaders were women.[8] And, in 2015, Deakin Business School found that 'women's representation in ASX leadership [was] at an all-time high', with women representing 8.2 per cent of directors across all ASX companies, 4.9 per cent of senior executives, 4.2 per cent of CEOs and 13 per cent of CFOs.[9] I hope you can see where I am going with these stats. Julia's achievement was phenomenal, as a male or female, but it must be said, especially as a woman.

Incidentally, in terms of beliefs, I was no better. How was it that it didn't even cross my mind that such a statement reeked of discrimination? Why wasn't I up in arms, protective of what Julia was achieving? I felt for her, but I didn't know any better. Because, despite my drive, ambition and belief in 'all things female', I had grown up cloaked in societal norms and expectations of what a woman's role was too. I had yet to experience my own exposure to some of the 'fight' Julia had already gone through. At this stage in my career, I was cocooned safely, working with Julia and other supportive high-achieving women. My time was coming.

Surprising facts: not-so-cool facts about gender discrimination

- Women are 47 per cent more likely to suffer severe injuries in car crashes because vehicle safety features are designed with men in mind. This bias in design has serious consequences, especially considering that women's smaller frames, neck strength and seating preferences make them more vulnerable during accidents.[10]

- In the workplace, women are twice as likely to be mistaken for junior employees compared to men.[11]

- Only six countries give women legal work rights equal to men's.[12]

- A 2017 study by The Rockefeller Foundation reported that 25 per cent of Americans think we will colonise Mars before half of the Fortune 500 company CEOs are women (go figure!).[13]

- *The* Organisation for Economic Co-operation and Development's Facebook page observed that 'Women spend more than 2.5 times as much time on unpaid care and domestic work than men'.[14]

So what's changed?

How much have we truly advanced? We may dress as we please for work, but have our attitudes, beliefs, behaviours and actions seen the same progress? It's easy to celebrate the superficial freedoms. We've come far, yet the path to true progress demands that we keep questioning, keep pushing and never settle for just the appearance of change.

Milk in the fridge wasn't a priority, nor should it have been. It is a guarantee that no other CEO of a global company was questioned that Thursday night about milk in the fridge—or any other household item!

Fast track from the early 2000s to today, and I know similar questions concerning 'home responsibilities' are still posed to women leaders and executives. I know because you—the candidates I interview daily—tell me. You tell me when we meet at the interview and then as you are accepting the promotion or new job. You are not complaining either. Rather, you share this with me as a pleasing addendum to your 'home contact', magically maintaining all domestic expectations while striving to achieve professionally.

As women, we can't genuinely refute patronising assumptions that our jobs and responsibilities are not of equal merit or importance if, at the same time, we agree to keep up all 'our' household, family and caring responsibilities. The imbalance in both paid and unpaid labour isn't just a matter of statistics; it's a reflection of the deep-seated expectations that continue to tether women to an unequal footing in the workplace and society.

Women take on extra work duties, promotions and advancements, and the quid pro quo is, 'as long as you don't drop the ball with your other responsibilities'. Is it punishment, envy, naivety, guilt or fear? It's all of that. This is why it will take centuries until women are on par in the earnings and gender equity stakes.

Learning to ask for help at work and home is essential. We must also push back on any inference that our jobs are hobbies or in some way 'cute' and stop the bargaining and conditions, especially those we impose on ourselves. Embracing our roles with confidence and conviction is not just about asserting our presence; it's about recognising and honouring our worth. We need to stand firm against any diminishing language or attitudes that undermine our contributions. The real challenge lies in stopping the internal negotiations that limit our potential. By doing so, we affirm our own values and pave the way for others to do the same.

'I'm a fraud'

I was advancing well in my career and now held a general manager position. I was close to 40 and still loving my job and career! Although I was progressing, achieving significant goals and seemingly successful, at the same time I can't say I ever felt 'deserving'. In fact, I sometimes felt undeserving. I couldn't shake the feeling that things somehow came too easily to me. Or maybe it was something else. Whatever was lingering wasn't just about the ease of my achievements.

Now I know that feeling was of the imposter. It was the voice in my head that many women recognise, warning me that I could be 'exposed' at any moment.

The female ingrained and conditioned belief at the time was that we shouldn't be here, at work, at this level and achieving. And when we are here, it's by invitation only. The hidden message is: 'Be careful, mindful and don't outstay your welcome.' Our success can be short-lived ... and we can be punished for it.

I often thought my run would be short-lived. *They will find out I'm not that smart and not that good.* I felt lucky instead of fortunate. Now I understand I was fortunate, not lucky. I achieved because I tried, and what I earned was deserved. If only I had possessed this wisdom back then.

This next story begins just after the end of the financial year.

My boss, who also happened to be female (I did say I love working with women!), was taking a three-month sabbatical, leaving me with a unique prospect to take on more responsibility.

It was a wonderful opportunity, and both the (male) Chief Technology Officer (CTO) and I put our hands up. The position was assigned to me, and I didn't give it a second thought. This was mainly because I couldn't see how the CTO had the skills, knowledge or experience necessary to run a recruitment business effectively, especially in a short-term, hands-on capacity.

In hindsight, it was an interesting observation and a valuable lesson. It never crossed the CTO's mind that he might lack the necessary skills. Had he been given the opportunity, he would have winged it, delegated (likely to me) or done whatever it took to succeed—something many women in his position might hesitate to do. Shame on us for that. On reflection, I realise that even without the requisite skills, he probably would have made a success of it. There was no question that he was capable, and he had self-confidence—a confidence that women often struggle to muster.

I was thrilled to be given the role. With years of management experience behind me, I was both delighted and scared at the same time—a perfectly normal reaction, I told myself. Determined and motivated to do a great job, I set off with a clear vision and strategy.

Then came the first challenge: the management reports. The CFO had recently resigned and the accounts team now temporarily reported to the CTO. The reports were due at the same time every month. I had always been particular about receiving them on time for my team and now, with national responsibilities, it was even more crucial. They had never been late. Until now.

Not too perturbed at first, I sent a polite follow-up email to the CTO (yes, the one who didn't get the secondment). Then another. Three days later, I received a curt email informing me that the reports would be late, with no explanation or apology.

So, I walked over to see him. He was sitting in his office, reading *WIRED* magazine. His office door was ajar. I knocked on the door, but I didn't step inside. Instead, I popped my head around the door, peering in tea-lady-like, and enquired about the financial reports. I may as well have asked if he would like 'Earl Grey or English Breakfast, a biscuit perhaps... and how about those management reports?'

Without glancing up from his magazine, he informed me I would have to wait and that I could expect the reports in a few days. It was a power play. I recognise that now, but I didn't at the time. I tried my best to reason with him, softly and demurely, but he wasn't budging, arrogantly continuing to read the magazine.

I was at a loss. I liked our CTO, and our relationship had always been amicable. Or so I thought. Why was this happening? I was having none of it. I pulled the authority line and demanded the reports immediately. I was uncomfortable asserting myself so forcefully, and he was visibly uncomfortable receiving my assertion. In fact, he squirmed.

Reflecting on the situation, it's clear that his ego had gotten in the way of professionalism. But I also realised that I could have handled the situation differently. I should have been more assertive and confident from the outset, rather than apologetic and demure. Polite, respectful and professional, yes, but I deserved that appointment and I wasn't behaving like I did. I was acting like I was lucky—like I had fluked it and was out of my depth. So I couldn't blame him for responding in kind. We must teach others how to treat us by the way we carry ourselves. If we act with confidence and assertiveness, we are more likely to be treated with the respect we deserve.

Contemplating on this experience, I realise how deeply ingrained gender biases can be, even in situations where we least expect them. The CTO's behaviour was not just a power play—it reflected the broader societal expectations that often undervalue women's contributions, especially when they step into roles traditionally held by men. But this situation also taught me something crucial: empowerment begins with how we see and assert ourselves.

I walked into that role with the skills and experience needed to succeed, yet I let self-doubt and societal conditioning make me feel as if I had fluked it. This hesitation in asserting my rightful place only gave room for others to question my authority. The key takeaway here is that empowerment is not just about being given opportunities—it's about claiming them with confidence.

We must recognise our worth, own our successes, and demand the respect we deserve. When we do this, we not only break free from the constraints of gender biases, but also set a powerful example for others to follow. As women in leadership, our responsibility goes beyond just performing well; it includes challenging the stereotypes that hold us and others back. By standing firm in our abilities and confronting biases head-on, we pave the way for true equality in the workplace.

So, the next time you're given an opportunity, don't just accept it. Embrace it, own it and let the world know you deserve every bit of it. In doing so, you're not just advancing your career, you're contributing to a broader movement towards gender equity and empowerment.

'You've got balls'

Said to a female, this is *not* a compliment. To a male counterpart, yes, but not to a woman. It really means 'you are being assertive and I'm not comfortable with it'. Or 'what you are communicating to me feels like a male sort of vibe and conversation, but I don't know how to respond. It feels weird and not how I have pigeonholed you. I am not sure how to deal with it, so I'll just blurt out, "You've got balls"'.

I have been told this, to my face and behind my back, so many times now that it's boring. It has never been intended as a compliment. Never. There is one time that stands out the most. It was with the same CTO who tried to undermine me with the late management reports.

After the reports fiasco, our relationship limped along. My boss returned and I was back in my original role, sans authority over the finance team. This was a problem because the CTO started to make my life difficult. I relied on him to make my division efficient in many areas.

The games started. The CFO position had still not been replaced and the CTO was smart in making himself indispensable.

Reports were not 'overdue', but 'justifiably late'. Issues with payroll or IT in my division were not prioritised. The CTO was the king of political game-playing, making Machiavelli look like a pre-schooler. I, on the other hand, was the pre-schooler's blind, three-legged puppy. Zero read of the situation, oblivious to any danger and risk. Instead, I expended my efforts trying to please, appease and placate. It seemed I had learned nothing from the last experience, except how to lick my wounds.

Until it all became too much.

I couldn't figure out how to win or play the game. My energy was being diverted away from my job, and I was stressed. So, once again, I went to his office. It was a similar situation: his door was ajar (no *WIRED* this time, though) and there was again no acknowledgement when I made my presence known.

I wasn't meek this time: there was no tea, but also no confidence. I made the mistake of letting my emotions override my thinking, and I was aggressive. I had played into his hand, but he didn't come out that well either. People heard our heated and emotional conversation and some of the accurate assertions I placed on him. He threw some equally on-point observations back. It was ugly. As I left his office, I could feel my heart racing. This was not good. Then, the finale for all to hear, he yelled out *those* words: 'You've got balls.'

I was mortified and humiliated. The shame from grade 5—when I fought a boy in the playground—raced back into my mind (even though I had won). I wasn't meant to be fighting this battle.

I tried to spin it differently. Maybe it was a compliment? It wasn't. I reflected a lot. Was I being aggressive? Did I deserve the name-calling? (For the record, *no-one* deserves name-calling.) My ruminations continued. 'Do I need to work on my style and tone?' The whole ordeal made me feel unworthy and embarrassed. There were more psychological beat-ups and hours of negative self-talk and criticism.

Then I thought: *Was this meant to be a subtle suggestion that my success hinges on adopting male traits?* This not only challenged my sense of identity, but also perpetuated the stereotype that I needed to emulate men to be an effective leader.

The slur was an intended putdown. It worked. The discomfort and stigma stayed with me for a long time. Imagine the negative impact of my future workplace conversations, wanting to be assertive but second-guessing myself, especially with male colleagues. That went on for years. I started to apologise before contributing at meetings, thinking it would soften my approach. Instead, it made me look weak.

Looking back now, I can see that the issue with the CTO stemmed from his own insecurity and unprofessionalism. If only I had shrugged it off sooner, my professional development could have advanced so much more quickly. There's a hidden cost to diminished self-worth and self-doubt; they become weights that stunt personal and professional progress. Confidence may be intangible, yet its absence has noticeable heft.

The one strategy I didn't employ at the time was to enlist help. It never crossed my mind to ask for advice or to report the behaviours or confide in my boss. I would now advocate seeking assistance and advice and reporting such behaviours. It is a fine line knowing what is appropriate, what is normal business politics, what is game playing and what is out-and-out bullying and discriminatory behaviours.

Peta Credlin shares with me similar experiences, recalling times she was 'mocked and ridiculed' simply for being a woman. She noted, 'It was always "the woman thing" because they couldn't attack the runs on the board. Maybe it's because I'm not a diminutive woman and perhaps if I'd spoken more softly and if I didn't give the whole truth and whispered it behind their backs, instead of saying it to their face. Maybe then it would have been different.' Reflecting further, she added, 'Perhaps all of that in aggregate terms is confronting.'

Confronting, yes Peta … in an inspirational and enlightening way.

Julia Ross: societal pressure and ignoring the noise

I have the unique and privileged honour of having known Julia for many, many years. Even still, when I interviewed Julia for the book, I was reminded sharply of just how extraordinary a person she is and how remarkable her achievements are. What has always been clear to me is Julia's ability to block the negative.

Julia recalled a time when she was scrutinised on live TV. The interviewer asked if she did tuckshop duty, clearly trying to undermine her as a mother.

Julia responded with, 'Well, actually, no I don't do tuck. Instead, I deliver career speeches at the school, along with other senior members of the community.'

'That sort of inference — being accused of not doing your job as a mother on national TV — would crush a lot of women. We need to say to other women that it is okay — it's all right for your child not to see you behind the counter at the tuck shop.'

'But there aren't enough women who are willing to say that.'

'It is not to the detriment of the family, nor does it mean your child doesn't have a perfect childhood. Allow women to have some dreams and support them along the way.'

On reflecting on other people's negativity and ignoring the noise, Julia says, 'I give it a minute's amount of time thinking about it. A minute...'

> That sort of attitude takes courage (not balls) and courage doesn't belong to any gender.
>
> I might also mention, for the record, the journalist who interviewed Julia at the time was a woman.

I wish I had known back when I was at loggerheads with the CTO what I know now. I believe in being accountable and having self-awareness and reflection. It is one of my strengths. However, I often take too much responsibility when it's not due. If I had had the older me as a guide, the advice would have been to reflect and learn, have better control of my emotions, and not overreact, but equally I should have 'only given it a minute of my time. A minute ...' Silence the negative self-talk and wallow, and reinstate yourself back to your deserved and earned place.

For the record, when I am in the moment, I still don't know how to respond to such comments if they are spoken or inferred ... they still happen and catch me off guard. But I do know how to respond afterwards, when I am by myself. I no longer let them take root in my mind.

The biggest thing you can do to effect change is to be successful. If you get into a position of seniority, you can change other women's lives.

JULIA ROSS,
ON GENDER EQUALITY

Chapter 2

GENDER BIAS TODAY: STILL ALIVE AND WELL

In 2020 — that's right, not that long ago — a woman in the United States was told that she needed her husband's permission to get her tubes tied.

For obvious reasons, the story went viral. It certainly wasn't the law where she lived. It was the policy of the medical clinic that the woman attended. Hmm... I think we have a long way to go before discrimination becomes a distant memory. Why do women still struggle to be recognised as independent and in control of their own lives?

Surprising facts: today's less-than-savoury discrimination truths

- Workplace Gender Equality Agency (WGEA) research identified that 36 per cent of the gender pay gap is attributed to discrimination.[15]

- According to a report by the Association of American Medical Colleges, 'though women account for about half of all medical school graduates, they are overly represented in paediatrics, obstetrics and gynaecology, which are among the lower paying specialties'.[16]

- The global female labour force participation rate is just over 50 per cent and has remained fairly flat over the past three decades according to the World Bank Group.[17]

- 'Australia's gender pay gap is closing. But today's working women will be retired before it is fixed.'[18]

- Iceland is the only country to have closed more than 90 per cent of its gender gap.[19]

In Australia, the current workforce participation gap is 8.6 per cent compared to 13 per cent in 2012.[20] You may read that figure and think it doesn't seem too bad. Hold that thought.

World Bank Gender Data reports show Australia's female workforce participation rate is 61.5 per cent,[21] compared to around 30 per cent in 1966.[22] Again, an incremental improvement, albeit at a slow pace.

Where improvement hasn't occurred is in earnings. Women earn a million dollars less than men over a lifetime, are less likely to be promoted and are significantly underrepresented in higher executive positions within organisations—and certainly at the board level.

Thirty-six per cent of the gender pay gap is attributed to discrimination.[23] The rest is due to a range of factors, including the pressure on women to fulfil pre-ordained social and familial roles. The International Labour Organization describes the gender pay gap as 'today's greatest social injustice'.[24] It's hard to believe, in today's enlightened era, that discrimination still holds court.

But people confuse the new gender pay gap legislation (I'll discuss in detail in chapter 3) with 'equal pay', which has been in place for more than 50 years. You can see where I am going ... if we were unaware equal pay was already law, then yes, of course, discrimination is alive and well, front and centre.

One might wonder why discrimination and bias persist even when legal frameworks are in place to prevent and punish. The answer lies in the complex interplay between laws, social policy and societal attitudes. Legal measures, while necessary, are not sufficient to eradicate deep-seated prejudices and systemic inequalities. These biases are so ingrained in our collective consciousness that they operate subtly, evading the reach of legislation.

For instance, research shows that women are often steered into lower paying roles, regardless of the industry, a phenomenon known as 'occupational gender segregation'. These biases are perpetuated through cultural norms and workplace practices and seem resistant to change.

As for discrimination, the enforcement of laws is often inadequate. Legal remedies typically require the victim to come forward and prove their case, which can be daunting and fraught with personal and professional risks. Many cases of discrimination go unreported not necessarily because of a lack of legal avenues, but due to fear of retaliation or doubts of achieving meaningful resolution. This underreporting allows discriminatory practices to persist unchecked.

To truly address these issues, we must go beyond legal measures and actively work to change the underlying attitudes and structures that perpetuate inequality. This involves education, awareness and a commitment to fostering inclusive environments both in and out of the workplace.

How far have we really come?

In this chapter, I look at some recent real-life stories. These stories demonstrate the reality of women's lives today. Here they are, fresh off the press.

I wasted a manicure

I had a striking conversation with a young woman during a recent event. This conversation highlighted to me the persistent gender-based pressures that women face.

The event was a breakfast—ironically, for International Women's Day (IWD). Clients from varied backgrounds joined us: from senior human resources directors and executive assistants to CEOs, and more. One of the HR leaders was sick on the day and sent her HR advisor, Sally, in her place. I could tell Sally was a little nervous, so I sat next to her and we started chatting. When people are nervous like this, I always look for easy conversation topics to kick off from.

Sally's flawlessly manicured hands did it for me. I am an admirer of anyone who wears nail polish well, probably because I cannot be trusted beyond 12 hours with a manicure. I chip it quickly, and then I have the chore of removing it—a waste of a manicure.

Sally's manicured hands were perfect—not a chip in sight. Every cuticle was in check; each nail bed slicked in a coat of bold, blood red. I was mesmerised and commented admiringly. Tauntingly, Sally raised her immaculate hands and, with a mixture of self-appreciation and disappointment, said, 'Yes, it's a wasted manicure, though.' I shared her sentiments about manicures but felt it would be for vastly different reasons.

Intrigued, I listened on. As Sally started to share her story, despite the attempts at comedy, I could tell she was deeply deflated. Carrying an air of hopelessness, she told me that she had just been away with her boyfriend to celebrate their 2-year anniversary. Immediately, I knew where this was going.

She was convinced her boyfriend was going to propose that weekend. She even had the hashtags worked out: #nearlyweds and

#gettinghitched. We had a big chuckle as she held up her perfectly polished hand, sans ring.

'Did he know what your expectations were?' I asked.

'No,' she replied.

'So,' I asked, 'where to from here?'

'I guess I'll have to wait and drop big hints,' she said, laughing slightly nervously.

Such tales have been commonplace for centuries, and almost every female I have ever met tells a similar one, including yours truly. They are indistinguishable: the girl waiting for the boy to propose at his convenience; the build-up, the manicures, waxes, hair; the disappointment; and then, the internal doubt and questioning. After all, *you* are waiting to be chosen, and it is all on *their* terms.

The conversation then shifted to the not-so-frivolous. We started talking about careers. I discovered that Sally was bright, smart, ambitious and determined. She had a degree, loved her job, and wanted to further her career in the learning and development space. Eventually, Sally wanted to move into leadership coaching. She recognised she needed more experience and extra study, so she had enrolled to study psychology part-time. She was impressive, and I could see why her boss had sent her that day.

This put my mind in a quandary. Here Sally and I were, at a breakfast for IWD, advocating and pushing for change and progress. At the same time, we were reverting to a fairytale of being rescued. I expected today's savvy 20- and 30-somethings to pave their own way, including in the proposal stakes. Granted, we can still seek the fairytale romance, but what holds us so firmly to this way of thinking? Why can't we buy our own ring and do the proposing?

There is nothing wrong with marriage. My argument is not against the institution itself, nor the idea of romance. Quite the contrary, the allure of romance and the shared myths give relationships meaning. Rather, it is about the societal norm imposed from childhood on how marriage and proposals play out.

Women are conditioned to accept it's up to the man to propose and invest so much in the idea of waiting to be chosen. Does this attitude, then, bleed into other areas of women's lives where they are always waiting and not initiating?

Reflecting on my conversation with Sally, it's clear that while we celebrate progress, old expectations still have a big impact. True empowerment goes beyond work achievements. It's about redefining our self-worth and abilities on our own terms. We need to let go of seeking approval from others and appreciate our own value.

I just hope Sara marries well

Shortly after celebrating International Women's Day, I overheard a candid conversation between two women on a train. The carriage was quite full, so I was surprised they were speaking so openly, but then I realised everyone else was glued to their phones and devices. Except me. I was glued to doing what I love: observing, or perhaps in this case, eavesdropping.

One lady, sitting in the aisle seat, enquired after 'Sara'. I worked out quickly that 'Sara' was the other lady's daughter, and had recently graduated with a marketing degree (congratulations, Sara!). It also appeared that Sara struggled with her studies, failed a few subjects and that it was touch-and-go whether Sara would graduate at all.

Sara's mum then said, despairingly, 'I just hope she marries well.'

At first, I thought she was joking. I sort of looked up a bit, waiting for the shared laughter. But no—she wasn't joking. Now I was intrigued.

So was the lady in the aisle seat, it appears, as she asked her friend the question I was dying to ask: 'Why don't you want Sara to have a career?'

Sara's mum said something like, 'I do, but I know how hard it is. She has her degree, and we are grateful she made it through. She is smart, but I don't want her to experience what I have been through in my career. I am tougher. We just want her to have a good life.'

I was surprised—shocked, even. In the 19th century, education was pursued not to empower daughters but to ensure they married well, to make them better wives and mothers. The goal wasn't independence but to mould women into being more accomplished and appealing. And here we are in the 21st century, still relying on a similar script. We continue to hope for a 'rescue' rather than fostering self-reliance and independence.

I understand that we want to protect other women from experiencing what we have gone through, especially those we care about. We would rather shelter those we love from having to bear similar burdens.

However, I also wondered whether the comment reflected a residual impact of traditional gender roles. These roles have long dictated that a woman's security and success are tied to her marital status. Despite her own career, Sara's mum may subconsciously be perpetuating these norms, reflecting a protective instinct to ensure her daughter's security in a world where gender biases still exist.

It's evident that our instinct to protect those we love can sometimes undermine their empowerment. As we strive to shield the next generation from life's challenges, we must also foster their ability to recognise and harness their own strengths. By doing so, we create a world where women don't just wait for support or permission but stride forward with the self-reliance and confidence that it's been theirs all along.

That's how life works

Recently, I had a conversation with Jon, a long-time client and friend. Jon owns a successful mid-sized property-development firm. We often discuss our shared business challenges. This time, we delved into the topic of succession planning, a critical issue for any growing business.

Jon's business is male dominated, although he strongly advocates for women and has employed several women in senior positions. As we talked, I expressed my challenges with succession planning in a female-majority workforce.

'Women,' I said, 'are still often seen as the primary homemakers and caregivers, which can make our "paid" jobs play second fiddle.'

Jon nodded, seemingly subconsciously accepting and agreeing with these societal expectations. Intrigued by his response, I continued probing and, admittedly, provoking a little.

'What's more,' I said, 'women also face the issue of husbands who are uncomfortable with their wives earning more or having demanding careers. So their job, career and the responsibilities that come with these can be way down the priority list, making it hard for women to realise their potential.' Jon's nod this time was one of wholehearted agreement, reflecting a pragmatic approach that many men share.

'Well, I guess that's how life works,' he said.

This response, though almost expected, underscored a critical point for me: societal norms deeply influence business dynamics. Even with the best intentions, as I have always seen with Jon, these norms can hinder women's career progression. I wanted to push the conversation further. So I did.

I asked Jon if he ever considered how these expectations shape the opportunities available to women in his industry. He paused, reflecting on the question, and his face revealed a mixture of realisation, embarrassment and concern. He then said words to the effect of, 'I've always believed in supporting women, but yes, you are right, these societal pressures are very much at play and do hold women back. It's not just about creating opportunities; it's about changing the environment that causes women to feel their careers are secondary.'

Our conversation highlighted another layer of complexity: the internalised beliefs women carry. Many women, conditioned by societal expectations, might not even strive for higher positions, anticipating familial and social pushback. This self-limitation can be just as powerful a barrier as external obstacles.

Reflecting on our conversation, it became clear to me that while there is awareness of these issues, deeply ingrained cultural expectations and biases continue to hold women back. As Jon and

I finished our catch-up, I couldn't help but think that the first step in solving these problems was having honest, open conversations like the one we had just had.

Change begins with awareness, but it flourishes through action. I am grateful to work with clients such as Jon.

Smart girl in the sauna

I've taken up the healthy habit of ice bathing. It is called 'contrast therapy' and involves alternating between sweating in a Swedish-style sauna and then immediately plunging into an ice bath for 3 to 5 minutes. This cycle continues for an hour. The icing is no mean feat and does involve some coaching. I had coaching when I started and was very grateful for it.

One day, I was sitting in the sauna and an attractive young lady (early 30s) came in. She was bikini-clad, and she told me she hadn't iced bathed before. I started chatting to her and gave her some advice. I helped her with her breath technique for the first couple of plunges. She did well.

Soon after, a 30-something gent joined us. Let's call him Jeffrey. He is Finnish and well-versed in saunas. We started chatting about the different varieties and methods of Europe versus the United States. It was obvious he was trying to impress bikini girl, until she posed some smart questions, mainly about the research data from the States not being calibrated. It was an impressive question, and legitimate. Always the curious recruiter, my thoughts were that she must work with numbers or analytics.

Instead of answering the question and setting up a rapport, Jeffrey waved his hand dismissively, saying something like, 'as if they would do that'. He then turned his attention back to me. We continued our conversation. It might seem as though he was intimidated by the question and wanted to fob her off. But he wasn't.

Having interviewed enough people, I know what intimidation looks like and this wasn't it. Here's my take: as someone nearly old enough to be Jeffrey's mother, my contributions were automatically respected. The smart girl in the bikini, however, didn't fit into Jeffrey's preconceived notions of who should offer insightful contributions. He didn't expect that cerebral level of participation from her and didn't know what to do with it.

At times like these, I wish for some super cool invention where I can press pause, rewind, remove bikini girl and replace her with Speedo boy. Let Speedo boy have the conservation about data, research and calibration and see how Jeffrey responds. My bet? The outcome would be very different.

Perhaps this is the tech tool we need, a hypothetical gadget to confront and deal with perceived discrimination and bias. By a simple press of a button to swap perspectives, we see the world through a different lens. Or we could rely on something low-tech, like self-awareness?

The young woman did not appreciate being dismissed, but she said nothing. I turned my attention back to her, continuing our conversation, hoping to encourage her smart thinking and repair any loss of confidence. She seemed okay, and not too perturbed, probably because she is used to these micro-occurrences and just swipes them away like an annoying mosquito. Of course, it was a given that Jeffrey was not successful in engaging in any further conversation with bikini girl.

Looking at this exchange, it's obvious that stereotypes and biases still manage to sneak in, shaping how we act, even for the much younger generations. Jeffrey's dismissive response to the young woman's insightful question highlights a pervasive issue: the undervaluation of contributions based on gender and age. While the young woman seemed unfazed, it's crucial to recognise that such small underestimations accumulate, eroding women's confidence and perpetuating inequality.

Another smart girl in the sauna: 'I surf a shortboard'

My obsession with ice bathing even follows me on holidays. As an incidental benefit, saunas turn out to be fascinating places for observing human behaviour. On the north coast of New South Wales, I have found a gym that provides contrast therapy. There, I made friends with Sam, the 30-something-year-old who manages the saunas and ice baths.

Sam is a gorgeous, sun-soaked blonde — tanned, friendly and super nice. She learned my name on the first day and we developed a rapport. As I sat sweating patiently in the sauna, I did what I always do: I observed. The sauna and ice baths are mostly frequented by males, and they all love Sam.

It's a constant chat-fest. One unlucky fellow started chatting with Sam about the surf. So far, so good: Sam surfs. Maybe I have the advantage, thanks to many years of doing my job, of reading tone, signals, body language and the like, but it was obvious to me that Sam is an accomplished surfer. Her physique, the answers she provided and her nonchalant responses suggest this. Sam knows her stuff.

They discussed the best surf spots, not just on the north coast but in Western Australia as well. Then the young man foolishly came out with, 'You surf a longboard.'

It was not a question. It was a statement, an assumption.

In surf talk, a longboard is more of a cruiser ride and easier to paddle. A shortboard is more manoeuvrable but less buoyant and harder to stay on, requiring more effort to paddle out and thus a higher level of fitness and skill. Longboards are for small, gentler waves, whereas shortboards excel in more powerful surf. You can see where I am going with this.

Sam's reply was curt. 'I surf a shortboard.' Conversation over, never to be revisited again, except for a feeble, last-ditch attempt by said male.

'Oh yeah ... that's cool.'

Sorry, mate. It's too late, I'm afraid.

As I witnessed this brief exchange, I couldn't help but think about how many times I have seen women being diminished by similar patterns of behaviour, not just in conversations about surfing but in other aspects of life. While these moments could be small and short, they accumulate, chipping away at confidence and reinforcing the biases that they originate from.

Sam chose to respond in a way that sent a quiet message of defiance. It was impactful and reminded me that we do not need to confront assumptions or agree to accept them. Rather, we can choose to define ourselves on our own terms. It's not about the volume of our voices. The power lies in the clarity of our convictions.

This seemingly insignificant exchange between Sam and the surfer speaks volumes. Even in the most casual of settings, these ingrained stereotypes reveal themselves, often in ways that are as subtle as they are pervasive. The young man's assumption about Sam's surfing ability wasn't just a misguided guess, it reflected deeper societal conditioning that leads to underestimation, especially in fields traditionally dominated by men.

Sam's response made her more formidable. This story isn't just about surfing. It's a reflection of the much greater hurdles women face almost daily. Whether in the boardroom, on the surfboard or in life, the challenge isn't just to prove ourselves but to navigate a world that often fails to see women clearly.

Peta Credlin on women backing themselves

'Women talking themselves out of opportunities...no amount of legislation is going to fix that.'

In our conversation, Peta and I delve into the layered issues of the gender pay gap and self-worth. She says to me, 'I think many businesses now go out of their way to ensure there is a pool of female talent. Yet, it's one thing to be told, like in politics to run for a seat. It's another thing to think you are worthy of putting your hand up, worthy of winning the seat and worthy of holding the seat.' She observes that, 'We are now less about dealing with the overt mechanisms holding women back and more about the covert ones.'

As she recounts her experiences, Peta provides vivid examples that bring her point to light. She tells me about a time in 2013, stepping into government and going from 80 to 500 staff. 'There were a lot of women putting their hands up for advisor roles, but very few putting themselves forward for senior advisor positions and they were absolutely capable at that level.' Peta told me she wanted to put a few of them forward for chief of staff, but they felt it 'was too much too quickly', or 'were not sure how they would juggle family commitments' or 'didn't want to look too big for their boots'.

Listening to Peta, I couldn't help but feel she had been privy to thousands of similar conversations I've had with women, often echoing the same responses.

Then the conversation took on another layer. Peta noted, 'I've hardly ever come across any bloke who, if I'd said, "You've applied for the advisor role, but I'm going to put you up for chief of staff or senior advisor", would knock it back or feel unsure or hesitate. It wasn't even that they were grateful for being offered a chance to step up. They are just sitting there as though I finally realised their brilliance. The women, on the other hand, they were grateful, reluctant and often needed to be convinced.'

She concludes with an insight that is as profound as it is frustrating: 'To be honest, I received more trepidation from women when I wanted to leapfrog them up the career ladder than willingness to take it on. And with the men, I don't remember ever having one of them knock back the opportunity. I guess for the women, it really came down to not seeing or valuing their worth.'

So what's the verdict?

Gender discrimination and bias still exist. They can be silent and unseen. Carrying the burden of inadequacy as well as lack of self-worth and self-belief into the working environment only begets further insecurities. The cycle continues. Females discovering their potential will unleash a surplus of opportunity for work and life, but most importantly, financial security.

The stories in this chapter showcase how we interact daily: carrying our gender assumptions, biases and conditioning and yet, absurdly, doing this in the era of our greatest awareness and awakening. Today, even in our seemingly advanced world, we are conditioned to it. It affects how we respond and behave, even for those of us who are aware and advocate equality.

I see and witness gender biases daily. I am trained to. It can be a tone, a single word, a gesture. Nothing over the top, but enough to send a subtle message. On most occasions, it is not intentional, with the sender obliviously unaware. Yet, with such hidden, deeply entrenched bias and discrimination, we can expect another 50-plus years to go by before we see any significant change.

The aim of sharing these stories is not just to highlight instances of bias, but to shine a light on the subtle yet influential forces that shape our perceptions of ourselves, of others and of the world around us. Biases, whether they arise in a casual conversation or at work, are akin to the undercurrents of a river: they guide the course of our interactions in ways we often overlook.

In sharing these moments, we begin to unravel the intricate web of influences that rules our behaviours and beliefs. We see how easily assumptions can limit our understanding, how readily we accept the roles assigned to us and how these roles, though comfortable, often confine us. But these stories also remind us of our capacity to challenge these forces, to rewrite the scripts we've been handed and to assert our own truths.

By becoming better attuned and aware, we can effect change, even if only in small ways. Encourage and empower instead of protecting; stand up, speak up, show support and don't slide into the background.

Oh, did I mention gender bias doesn't just sit with males? Women do this to women as well. As a checkpoint, who is your doctor, dentist, lawyer or accountant? Who would you prefer as your pilot, and what about the police you call out in the middle of the night? Reflect on your answers. They could tell you a lot.

I kind of took destiny into my own hands. I think this is what we all need to do. If we can't change the legal system and the pay gap is so big, we can't just sit around waiting for it to happen.

KRISTINA KARLSSON,
ON THE MILLION-DOLLAR
GENDER PAY GAP

Chapter 3

FEMALE WORTH: THE REALITY OF THE GENDER PAY GAP

If you are an Australian working woman, it's likely you earn about 22 per cent less than the average Australian male worker. What's more, at the current rate, it will take 257 years to close the gender pay gap.[25]

'She's Price(d)less' is a series of reports that explore the gender pay gap. It is produced by the Workplace Gender Equality Agency (WGEA), in conjunction with the Diversity Council Australia (DCA) and KPMG. I fell in love with the cleverness of the title straight away. Looking past the pleasure derived from brilliant wordsmithing, this apt title is the workforce reality for women.

Using econometric modelling, the report unpacks the factors contributing to our gender pay gap, being the difference between the average earnings for men and women, expressed as a percentage of men's average earnings. According to the findings, Australia's total remuneration pay gap is 21.7 per cent. So, for every $1 a man earns, a woman earns 78 cents.[26] The gender pay gap issue is not unique to Australia. The *Global Gender Gap Report 2023* conducted by the World Economic Forum affirms that the gender pay gap score stands at 68.4 per cent globally.[27]

Surprising facts: the reality of the gender pay gap

- Men have a higher salary than women in 95 per cent of all occupations.[28]

- The gender wage gap persists in nearly every occupation.[29]

- The United States is one of only four countries that don't guarantee paid maternity leave. Congress has attempted to fix this by tinkering with Social Security, but its efforts only reduced benefits for women.[30]

- The *Workplace Gender Equality Amendment (Closing the Gender Pay Gap) Bill 2023* is not about equal pay for the same job.

- Equal pay for doing the same job became law in Australia in 1969 — more accurately, in 1972.

If you are sceptical and looking for an angle to defy the statistics, don't waste your time. All the research and reports point to similar findings. In the United States, according to the Pew Research Center, the gap in earnings between men and women has 'barely closed in the last two decades'.[31] United Nations data shows that, globally, women earn, on average, 77 cents for every dollar earned by men. The data also predicts that at current estimates, it will take 257 years to close the gap.[32]

Perhaps you prefer a disaggregated view. According to the *Global Gender Gap Report 2023*, at the current rate of progress, it will take '162 years to close the political empowerment global gender gap'.[33] Not to be outdone, the World Economic Forum 2023 contends that 'parity has advanced by only 4.1 percentage points since the first edition of the report in 2006, with the overall rate of change slowing significantly'.[34] Not only that, but it estimates that it will take '169 years for economic parity and 162 years for political parity'.

If you want to hone in on discrimination and discrepancy in all their glory, look no further than the intersectionality of the pay gap. In 2023 the Pew Research Center reported that '[i]n 2022, Black women earned 70 per cent as much as White men, and Hispanic women earned only 65 per cent as much'.[35] *Missing Perspectives* reports that the ethnic pay gap for Australian organisations can be around 33 to 36 per cent.[36]

Since 2024, Australia's gender equality legislation (the *Workplace Gender Equality Amendment (Closing the Gender Pay Gap) Bill 2023*) requires organisations with more than 100 employees to publish their pay gaps via the WGEA website. The purpose of this is to raise awareness and to ensure transparency on gender equality in the workplace.

Closing the gender pay gap should not be confused with the principle of 'equal pay for equal work', which became law in Australia in 1969 (and which was revised in 1972 'to encompass "equal pay for work of equal value", with a single rate for a job, regardless of gender').[37]

Many people assume the 2023 Bill is also about equal pay, and it is precisely this lack of awareness that sees us still in a dire gender pay gap situation today.

I have discovered that most gender issues—especially those surrounding pay gap discrepancies—reek of conditions, loopholes and tests. The perfect example is the equal pay law introduced in 1969.

In 1969, the Australian Conciliation and Arbitration Commission (ACAC) ruled that a national award minimum wage for women be established at '85 per cent of the male wage'.[38]

Equal pay indeed! However, the decision did allow for equal pay in some instances where a job was assessed as consisting of exactly the same duties as those of men in traditionally male roles. The benchmark example was women working in an abattoir handling meat. I mean … could there have been a more extreme or obscure example for the allowance?

What if you weren't handling meat? Well, if you were a woman working in an abattoir with the accounts team back in 1969, it was almost guaranteed that the male you were sitting next to, doing the same job, was being paid more. Or let's put it this way, 'luckily'—because of the new law—you would be earning no less than 85 per cent of whatever he earned. And that's only if his role wasn't conveniently reclassified as more senior, or slightly different—perhaps with a new title. Make no mistake, these tactics were common.

Even after the revision of the law was passed in 1972, there was no magic wand or fairy dust. In fact, here we are today, fighting a similar fight disguised differently. At its core, this is about women's worth. It's a shame I was only one year old then. I want to believe I would have been out there protesting for women's rights. Or maybe not; maybe I would have been conditioned to be grateful and patient, just like all the other women. I hope not.

So, for absolute transparency, the discrepancy in gender pay refers to the gap in (significant) earnings due to systemic and societal structures. These structures go unseen and are insufficiently challenged.

The WGEA estimates that, over their lifetime, women earn a million dollars less on average than men and retire with $136000 less in superannuation.[39] These are not figures to be ignored or complacent about.

The WGEA's gender pay discrepancy figure is based on factors such as female-dominated industries with jobs attracting lower wages. Feminised industries—such as healthcare, social assistance, education and training, and retail—face barriers to achieving wage parity. Additionally, a substantial contributing factor is that women also spend less time in the workforce due to caring or family responsibilities. From my own workplace observations, I have similar estimates. But I'll come to that.

Surely women in leadership roles are immune?

They're not. 'Women in the top 20 per cent of income earners experience the largest gender pay gap' at 18 per cent.[40] Overwhelmingly and inescapably, '36 per cent of the gender pay gap [is] due to gender discrimination'.[41] My own experience as an employment expert confirms this to be undoubtedly true, and those at the top end are not immune.

For senior—let's call them career-based—roles, a 2024 University of Melbourne study found that women make up only 22 per cent of CEO positions, 37 per cent of key management roles and 34 per cent of board positions;[42] and the WGEA reports that they occupy only 19 per cent of chair roles.[43] So, it's fair to say that one driver of the gender pay gap is the type of job. In other words, if more men hold high-paying positions, the data will naturally reflect a pay discrepancy. It seems logical—until you realise that even at senior levels, where women should be on equal footing, the gap still persists.

And it gets worse. Let me introduce you to the 'glass cliff' effect,[44] where studies suggest that women are disproportionately appointed to precarious leadership positions in struggling organisations or challenging environments. Meanwhile, men are more likely to be appointed to stable leadership positions in successful organisations. With a higher rate of failure in the precarious leadership positions, the prophecy is fulfilled and the fallacy continues. While this pattern is observed in various studies, it is important to note that leadership dynamics can vary across industries and cultural contexts.

If you think I'm joking, please do the research. Better still, look around you. There are many prominent examples to illustrate this point. In recent times in Australia, we have seen Michele Bullock replace Dr Philip Lowe as the Reserve Bank Governor,

Vanessa Hudson replace Alan Joyce as CEO of Qantas, Amanda Bardwell take over from Brad Banducci at Woolworths and Leah Weckert take the lead at Coles, to name a few.

Internationally, look no further than the UK, with Theresa May taking on the leadership role of the conservative party for Brexit negotiations. Or the very short-lived appointment of Liz Truss as UK's Prime Minister for only 45 days. Given these examples, it's perhaps less surprising that women only hold 26 per cent of parliamentary seats worldwide,[45] an unfortunate lack of fair representation where it is sorely needed. On this point, though, I can't help but think it's women truly showing how smart they are.

When Liz Truss stepped down, my immediate thought was, *No! It will make women look poor in the leadership stakes — as though we can't cut it.* I, too, fell into the well-laid trap. It was my partner who pointed out to me that maybe Liz was smart to get out. His words: 'Why would she put herself through working in a toxic environment like that?' An apt description.

This begs another question: Why was my automatic response that women should tough it out as though we have something to prove? *Sadly, because it's instilled in us.* This mindset has been deeply ingrained in me through my own experiences. I am fortunate in my career and where I am professionally; however, it doesn't come without some fight, its own baggage, scars and yet-to-be-healed wounds.

Michelle Ryan from the Global Institute for Women's Leadership and professor of social and organisational psychology at the Australian National University, along with Alex Haslam from Exeter University, first came up with the term and concept of the 'glass cliff' phenomenon I mentioned earlier. There is the argument that progress is evident when we see women in these senior, if not precarious, roles. Michelle Ryan counters that 'if they are more likely to be in such positions in times of crisis, we run the risk of reinforcing stereotypes of women not being good in leadership roles.'[46] She's right.

Having women in senior and executive roles is vital. At the leadership and executive level, it provides women with a voice and inspiration, enabling awareness and change. Sheryl Sandberg, in her book *Lean In*, famously talks about marching in to see her boss, Sergey Brin, and demanding the company create closer pregnancy parking for expectant mothers. Brin immediately said yes and wondered why such an idea had never occurred to him. Sandberg comments, 'As one of Google's most senior women, didn't I have a special responsibility to think of this? Having one pregnant woman at the top made the difference.'[47]

Julia Ross once said to me, 'The biggest thing you can do to change the gender dynamic is to be successful.' When we spoke about the importance of women in leadership, her comments were altruistic and for the greater good of women. 'Get yourself into a position of seniority so you can employ, sponsor and mentor other women. Then you can change women's lives. That's what I have always tried to do.'

The omnipresent gender pay gap

Here's an interesting fact: even when there is evidence of change or a move in the right direction, the gender pay gap stubbornly remains. No matter the industry or country, the gender pay gap attributes a fair proportion of the discrepancy to women in lower paying jobs such as cleaning, social work, health and teaching. (This might be true, but I always felt the reason to lean weakly on some superficial level.) The solution? Education was proffered as the golden egg to bridging the pay gap. As I thought, it isn't enough.

In the United States, women have more years of education than men and are more likely than men to have completed undergraduate or postgraduate degrees. Yet the US Women's Bureau observed that the gender pay gap remains evident at every educational level.[48] In 2022, 'women with a bachelor's degree earned 79 per cent as much as men who were college graduates',[49] and worse, the pay gap widens as the educational level increases, according to *Statista*.[50]

In Australia, 61 per cent of bachelor-degree graduates and 55 per cent of new PhD and masters research graduates are women.[51]

Still, women are behind. Female graduates are earning $3000 a year less than their contemporaries. At the postgraduate level, men will earn $13 000 more than women with the same qualification, a difference of 12.4 per cent, maintains the Financial Review.[52]

The counterargument has always been that the discrepancy is due to the industries women choose to work in. Apparently, women are not doing enough study in science, technology, engineering and maths (STEM skills). Again, I question the validity of the argument. It is another hoop to jump through: 'Here: do this, and *then* we will pay you the same.'

I have always lacked conviction that changing the jobs women do will make enough of a difference—and here we are. The 2023 Graduate Outcomes Survey unveiled that the occupations with the highest gender pay gaps for undergraduates were 'architects and built environments with a gap of $8000 and medicine with $6700'.[53] Last time I checked, you need maths and science to do these jobs.

Before World War II, the role of the secretary was prestigious, and one that was carried out mainly by men. You can see the remnants of this in political titles such as 'Secretary of State'. However, when so many men were sent off to fight during the war, women had to step in and take over as secretaries. As a result, the role of secretary became less prestigious because it had been feminised.

Often, it is not a matter of a man's role being intrinsically worth more because it is more complex or requires higher skills. It is a matter of the role being considered worth more *because it is more frequently performed by men* and because we continue to live in a society where there is a tacit assumption that the way a man spends his time is worth more money than the way a woman spends hers. As Paula England, a sociology professor from New York University, pointed out, 'once women start doing a job … gender bias sneaks in'.[54] That's our truth.

Need more proof? *The New York Times* reported that when women enter fields in larger numbers, their income is reduced for the same jobs men were previously doing. So, when women in large numbers become designers, wages fall 34 percentage points. For housekeepers, the drop is 21 percentage points and for biologists, 18 percentage points.[55] What about jobs that require similar education and responsibility levels but are typically divided by gender—such as human resources managers (female) and information technology managers (male)? According to the Bureau of Labor Statistics, the average salaries for information technology managers are 27 per cent higher.[56]

Discrimination and discrepancy aren't just reserved for the senior end either. Male cleaners (janitors) in the United States 'earn 22 per cent more than maids and house cleaners' (usually female).[57] It doesn't matter where the data is based. Discrimination and wage discrepancy are global issues that cross all borders and boundaries.

As if it is not enough that women earn less than men, our wealth creation is also sadly in dire need of help. The wealth gap, as it is referred to, is 'less well known'.[58] Of course it is. It's too much of a good thing, so we'd better keep it quiet! According to a Merrill Lynch report, *Women and Financial Wellness: Beyond the bottom line*, the average single woman has three times less wealth than the average single man. The report talks about women having less access to wealth accelerators and the opportunity to invest.[59] But how can you invest if you don't have the disposable income to do so? Not having a 22 per cent difference in earnings would go a long way to assisting the situation.

That's 22 cents for every dollar. Using the average Australian salary of \$98 217, 22 cents equates to upwards of \$21 607 a year according to the Australian Bureau of Statistics (ABS)[60]. I recognise that I am oversimplifying the situation and the numbers, but there is merit in the story. It's compelling, and I'm confident most of us would welcome an extra \$21 607—let alone a million dollars over a lifetime.

Social ramifications

Bridging the gender pay gap has far-reaching and serious societal ramifications. The connection with women in poverty cannot be underestimated. Women's ability to earn is becoming increasingly important for all facets of security and stability: economic, emotional, psychological and physical. It also affects children, with their safety and welfare being a priority.

Women are far more likely to experience poverty than men. More women than men live in poverty, and 14 per cent of all women in Australia live below the poverty line.[61] According to the United States Census Bureau's official poverty measure, in 2021 '11.7 per cent of women' were living in poverty and '5.6 per cent were living in extreme poverty',[62] which is defined as living on less than the international poverty line (IPL) of just \$2.25 a day.

Closing the gender pay gap plays a crucial role in liberating women and children from violence. Simply put, it gives women a way out. In Australia, one in four women experience violence from an intimate partner. According to the World Health Organization (WHO), 'about 1 in 3 (30%) of women worldwide have been subjected to either physical and/or sexual...violence'.[63] The Australian Longitudinal Study on Women's Health states that 'sexual violence is consistently associated with high financial stress'.[64]

The gender pay gap not only perpetuates women's inequality, it entrenches the disadvantage of cultural groups who experience ongoing discrimination and disadvantage. Women in Australia have demonstrated great strength and resilience in dealing with adversity. This is particularly true for Aboriginal women. Some of Australia's most prominent women advocates, activists and public figures are First Nations people such as Megan Davis, an international human rights lawyer and the first Indigenous Australian to sit on a United Nations body.

I don't want to bore you with data, research and facts, but this cannot be a subjective argument. Women are on the raw receiving end of what is fair, morally right and just. The repercussions go beyond a cursory consideration.

Our work is not as highly valued as that of men, perhaps even by ourselves. Women, as a collective, can effect change faster than any legislation. After all, I don't know many women who do not aspire to leaving a positive impact on the younger generation, providing a sense that others have benefited from our presence in this world.

Don't lure yourself into thinking that this is just an economic issue. It is also a moral one. In that sense, we see the gender pay gap as a reflection of how we value, and undervalue, approximately half of our population.

When revealing the reality of the gender pay gap, numbers and statistics don't simply represent figures. They represent people. They are the reality and life story of numerous women. Insisting on the importance of the gap is not only about the dollars and cents women are missing out on. It is much more about the opportunities lost, the potential unfulfilled and the autonomy compromised.

The value of the data and shared experiences could sometimes be overwhelming, and this is where the paradox lies because it also provides us with clarity. It takes away any illusions about how far we have come and shows us exactly where work still needs to be done.

If there were no hope, there would be no point in writing this book. Hope is more than a feeling; it is a catalyst for change. The best way to use that hope is not by criticising the world or regulations but by reflecting upon how we see our own value, how we advocate for ourselves and others and, finally, how we challenge the norms.

So, while the gender pay gap is a crucial topic in today's social and individual narrative, it is not just about closing the gap, but also opening the doors to endless opportunities for financial and psychological independence under our (women's) terms. To do that, we need to keep channelling the same amount of strength, resilience and determination that has brought us thus far. Most importantly, we owe it to ourselves, to those who came before us and to the generations that will follow.

Peta Credlin on self-worth

Throughout my interview with Peta, there are numerous stories showing her strong sense of self-worth, which should not be confused with self-confidence. She is someone who knows who she is and is comfortable in her own skin. My favourite and perhaps most endearing account is the one from when Peta first entered politics. Perhaps it's the recruiter in me, savouring these moments when people find their calling, or maybe it's because I felt the same way when I landed my first job.

Here is what Peta told me: 'Whatever life was going to be for me, I wanted a life of consequence. I wanted to live a brave life. And I was always willing, as a kid from a small country town, to do the hard work needed to get where I wanted to go. Over the years, I've learned to build a resilience. I've learned to let a lot of stuff wash over me that a few years ago I would have wasted time and energy worrying about. I now only invest my time where I can make a difference and then I throw everything I have at it.' She said, 'I finished my law degree and decided to take a job in politics writing speeches for Kay Patterson. It was only meant to be for 1 year and then I was going to go off and be a lawyer. I was in Canberra. It was maybe three or four weeks into the job, and someone asked me to improve a draft amendment that a tables office clerk had written. I did, and my changes carried on the floor of parliament.'

Peta said, 'I was like, are you kidding me? This is like someone who likes aviation and suddenly gets to sit next to the pilot and help land the plane. It was so exciting! From then on, you could have paid me nothing and I would have wanted to do that job. And I did, for the next 16 years as that one year turned into many.'

Fast forward and Peta's entrée into the world of media is similar. Peta said, 'I was only meant to be doing a short 6-week stint on the 2016 election campaign, that's all I agreed to, and it's now over 7 years. I am the perfect lesson in a career that's focused on what I want out of it and the sort of life I want to live, rather than a structured sort of plan.

'Part of my story, like so many women, is finding out who I am, who I want to be and what I stand for. And once you know that — who you are and what you stand for — then you've got to keep yourself honest and live the life you told yourself you wanted. I would feel that I had let myself down if I didn't speak-up on the things I care about. I am not afraid to shake the tree, I'm not afraid to take a risk, to fall and have to get up again. I've grown a tough skin over the years and come through some really difficult chapters like years of unsuccessful IVF. It's all part of my story — the successes and the failures, the ups and the downs. But what I am most proud of is that I gave it a go, that I won't be one of those who has a litany of regrets on their deathbed. I used to keep that wonderful quote from Eleanor Roosevelt on my wall at uni that said, 'no one can make you feel inferior without your permission'. And seriously, that's a quote for all of us women isn't it?'

I was never seduced by making millions or having an important title. I just wanted to live a really brave life. I wanted a life that made a difference.

PETA CREDLIN

Chapter 4

WHAT COULD YOU DO WITH $1 MILLION?

So now you know about the million-dollar gap in lifetime earnings. The next question is, what would you do with a million dollars?

No doubt the answer is, 'A lot.'

Reflect on the lives of your mother and grandmothers. What could they have done with a million dollars and how different would their lives have been? And, consequently, yours?

If your thoughts immediately go to the tangible: housing, cars and holidays, join the club. It is a natural and normal thought process and there's nothing wrong with that. However, earning a million dollars, in the context of gender-based discrepancies, brings far more profound benefits.

Go back to your mother and grandmothers for a moment, and forget the desire for 'nicer things'. What is the ultimate prize? Time. Anyone who has lost someone close to them understands this deeply. Time is one of life's most precious commodities and we all wish for more of it.

The million dollars? Well, being financially well off equates to better health and longer life expectancy. The surprising facts in this chapter list some shocking facts on this issue — specifically, about women's poverty and life expectancy.

This isn't just an Australian issue. Studies globally point to similar and equally alarming findings. Research suggests that in the United States, the life expectancy gap between the rich and the poor is increasing.[65] As time progresses, and with increased awareness and access to education, there are still no improvements in the life expectancy of women in the low-earning bracket, while for top earners, it has increased to more than 10 years.[66] This gap underscores a harsh reality: wealth buys not just comfort, but time.

More years of health, wellbeing and with loved ones. That's what you can do with your million dollars.

Surprising facts: wealth and health

- Over their lifetime, women earn a million dollars less than men.

- A study by the National Bureau of Economic Research reveals that '80 per cent of women struggle with low self-esteem and shy away from self-advocacy at work'.[67]

- Parents pay boys twice as much for doing chores per week.[68]

- By the age of 42, men are 34 per cent more likely to be in the top jobs than women, with overconfidence explaining 11 per cent of the gender gap.[69]

- In Australia, people with higher incomes (60 per cent) are more likely to report good health, while those with lower income levels (32 per cent) are less likely to report good health.[70]

Other profound benefits with generational impact

Equal earnings extend beyond merely a matter of fairness; it is a catalyst for unlocking every woman's boundless capabilities. The promise of financial parity fosters a sense of empowerment, allowing women to envision a future where their contributions are valued equally. The power of financial security is not just in the dollars, but also in the opportunities and freedoms. It provides assurance to reduce economic stress, make life decisions with greater security and optimism, and ultimately improve the quality of life.

Then there are the psychological benefits. From the very first steps that we take to control our financial future, we already begin to foster our self-esteem and increase our mental wellbeing, leading to greater self-confidence and empowerment. If that's not enough, in terms of the collective, if the workforce is more equitable, society witnesses a ripple effect of increased innovation, productivity and economic growth driven by a more motivated and diverse workforce.

So why aren't we more actively pursuing the million dollars?

The collective female acquiescence of earning less than men had always puzzled me. But then, I began to understand why...

We don't think the pay discrepancy applies to us.

It's our shared denial. It resembles Hans Christian Andersen's fable *The Emperor's New Clothes*. The pay disparity is the emperor's non-existent outfit, plainly visible yet widely ignored. Just as the emperor parades naked through the streets, the wage inequality struts before us, obvious, but unacknowledged. Head in the sand: 'It doesn't apply to us.'

Collective silence and self-deception allow the charade to continue. We pretend the emperor is clothed in magnificent garments, just as we pretend the workplace is a level playing field. It's more comfortable to believe the illusion than to confront the uncomfortable reality.

Society's illusion, our disillusion, everyone looking the other way, the pretence and self-deception. It manifests and continues. And so we convince ourselves again that 'surely this doesn't apply to us'.

I mean, I didn't think it applied to me! And I live, breathe, walk, talk, sleep and roll in it. Even if we concede that the pay discrepancy exists, we say it applies to 'those other women'. And there's no way it could add up to a formidable figure such as a million dollars. Instead, I'm sure we write it off, believing it to be an inconsequential amount: a few dollars, even a few thousand (it's not, by the way). We tell ourselves it's not worth the fight.

If we were to take a side glimpse at this truth for a moment and consider its legitimacy, we would go into denial.

The million dollars becomes more than an inconvenience: it is an obvious truth we would rather not confront. Like the emperor, we hold the mirror but refuse to look, paralysed by the fear of what we might see. It's not the absence of knowledge that blinds us, but the unwillingness to face it. And yet, deep down, we long for the clarity of the child who speaks the truth without hesitation: 'He isn't wearing anything at all.' In that simple act, the truth is set free—no longer hidden, no longer denied.

The child isn't being brave; it is innocence we are witnessing. No constraints and expectations of what we 'should' see. If only we adults could apply the same view to life, unencumbered and unrestrained.

Convincing ourselves we are all on equal footing highlights the cognitive dissonance (that is, 'the state of discomfort felt when two or more modes of thought contradict each other')[71] when confronting this issue. The uncomfortable tension that arises when our beliefs clash with reality, the push, pull and contradiction of our values at play.

Yet, when we test our assumptions, we:

- challenge outdated beliefs
- discover new truths
- make more informed and better decisions.

I tested it! The million dollars is legitimate

The calculations are correct. Our beliefs are outdated and our decisions must be smarter and more informed.

Make no mistake, women earn a million dollars less over their lifetime than men. This isn't a distant issue. It touches every woman somehow, shaping lives in ways both seen and unseen. This reality has been clear to me for a long time, yet its gravity never ceases to surprise.

Well before the 'She's Price(d)less' report and the WGEA findings, I calculated the gap in earnings to be $1 million … and counting. Each time a woman I knew declined a workplace opportunity, failed to claim the credit she deserved or didn't negotiate for better terms, I mentally tallied the lost dollars of what could have been. Even back then, the numbers came to $1 million.

My calculations eerily mirror the reports from the WGEA. My estimates are almost identical. (Chapter 5 details the estimates and different earning scenarios.) The causes are mostly the same. However, I have some differing thoughts and calls to action. The reports identify time off for caregiving responsibilities, attributing this to 33 per cent of the gender pay gap; female-dominated industries impacting 24 per cent;[72] and gender discrimination contributing 36 per cent to the gender pay gap.[73] Global reports back this up, showing similar findings and referring to it as 'implicit gender bias'.[74]

Discrimination: doubling down — that's what affects your earnings!

A 36 per cent gender-based discrepancy is alarming, yet it barely scratches the surface of discrimination's full impact on women. What's more alarming is the interplay of discrimination and gender bias on our attitudes, beliefs and decisions. The legacy gift we never asked for.

The continued impact of discrimination cannot be underestimated. Daily, we carry the residual impacts of discrimination and gender bias, and this affects the decisions we make. The decisions in the workplace that could see us $1 million ahead. This is where I anchor much of my focus, on what women can do to change the narrative and belief patterns to achieve financial parity. I also recognise that it's not so simple.

Discrimination in all its unfair and unjust forms is not isolated to our workplace. If only! If that were the case, it would be combatted much more easily. So striking would the injustice be that it could never be tolerated in an isolated environment such as at work. But instead, while encountering discrimination daily — what I call 'lived discrimination' — we've become so accustomed to it that we tolerate it, dress it up and disguise it as something else.

I know I do. Sometimes I don't even register it, or I brush it off like a bothersome piece of fluff. We are all so conditioned to accept it, but we should be questioning and rejecting it instead. 'Oh, that's just John! He doesn't mean anything by it.' Hmm, it's a justification and deep down, subconsciously, he does.

The real questions we need to ask are:

- What makes women think they are worth less?

- What compels them to downplay their potential and limit their own achievements?

- What deeper societal structures and beliefs are guiding this pattern?

Let's begin by examining ...

Subtle judgements and their effects

It isn't about that one instance of discrimination, whether big or small, a joke or not. It's the cumulative effect of bias, prejudice and intolerance. And that's big and no joke.

Just after completing my MBA, I caught up with an old (male) work colleague. We had both held divisional management positions in a previous company. He was driven and professional, and we always clicked on ideas, strategy and business approach. Not having seen each other for several years, we were having drinks and chatting about what was going on in our worlds.

I shared with him that I had just finished my MBA. (As an additional note, my MBA took me 5 arduous years, most weekends, personal and family sacrifices, and a lot of sweat, stress and the odd tear, so I was pretty chuffed I got through!)

His question back to me was, 'Did you do it online?' The inference was that I couldn't possibly have gone to a 'proper' business school and committed to the timings of its curriculum. Well, I did go to a 'proper' business school. His face said it all. The well-known expression of disbelief. His mind and eyes said this: 'How did *you* pull that off?'

Studying for an MBA had been a previous goal of his as well.

On reflection, it may have been a confronting fact and comparison. I know he didn't intend to belittle or patronise me — quite the opposite. He was likely unaware, so deeply ingrained were his belief systems and (gender) biases. Still, it didn't feel great. I should have been proud to celebrate my news and achievements.

If we wonder why more women don't self-promote, this could be why. Instead of receiving acknowledgement, a pat on the back and celebration, they often face judgement and a subtle push back into their 'place'.

I didn't challenge my friend, and I should have. My friend's statement was subtle: an implicit bias shaped by his unconscious beliefs. It is my experience that these are the hardest biases to call out and confront; the biases where the person doesn't seem to be unkind or doesn't even realise what they are saying. I believe they can be the most damaging and even dangerous. If you are on the receiving end, the impact can be devastating, especially when it's reoccurring ... time and time again. The fact I still recall it today—though it was only a fleeting conversation from years ago—says it all.

Biases from people we care about carry more weight. Their judgements cut deeper. These instances and experiences are more significant because they challenge our sense of self in a way distant opinions don't. Over time, these subtle messages from those we care about can influence our self-esteem because we seldom confront them openly, and therefore they stay silent within us.

You might question why I still call him a friend, but he was—and is—despite his unconscious slight. By the way, don't be too quick to judge. Many of you reading this have likely experienced the same.

Being on the receiving end of bias—implicit or otherwise—or discrimination—intended or not—from those you know or are close to—family, friends, colleagues and bosses—is so common, it's ubiquitous. Which is why it's an even harder conversation to have. But we must start having them!

Persistent, ongoing bias and prejudice leave lasting impressions, shaping our psychological and emotional framework. They are a constant and unwelcome shadow in every workplace interaction and negotiation. Holding you back, they exact a heavy toll, as shown clearly in our workplace decisions.

Internal forces and decisions we make

As a recruiter, I see women make work-related decisions every day. I've been studying these workplace choices for decades. Occasionally, I would be perplexed, thinking, 'Are you crazy? It's such an incredible opportunity. Why aren't you running with it?' Ultimately, though, I respected the decisions made by these women. I accepted the reasons, justifications and even excuses. However, as I continued to observe, the significance and ramifications of women's workplace decisions became increasingly clear. I saw the patterns, parallels and costly financial fallouts. Then I turned my view to the men I worked with. I analysed how they acted and treated themselves and the opportunities that came their way. The contrast was stark.

These are my observations:

- Women are more reluctant to take up workplace opportunities or put their hand up for advancements, or even at meetings for that matter.

- Women shy away from self-promotion; preferring to describe themselves as 'humble'.

- Women tend to avoid the spotlight.

- Women rarely go for a promotion unless they feel they 'can definitely do it'.

- Women don't take credit where they should.

The list goes on.

Women are not promoted at the same rate as men. But even when offered promotions, opportunities for growth and advancements:

- we are more likely to decline

- we think we can't do the job, promotion or training, so we don't. Others think we can't, so we don't. Or worse, others think we shouldn't, so we don't

- we half-heartedly try but lack faith in ourselves, so we give up when we should keep going

- we volunteer for responsibilities that don't lead to promotions

- we rarely back ourselves

- we also don't back each other enough (but that's another matter and the other fight we must engage in as a female collective).

We act this way because we lack self-confidence and self-belief, and what we lack in these areas, we make up for with ample self-doubt. These are the internal forces impacting our decision making.

> ### *Self-doubt is the number-one killer of every dream.*
> **Kristina Karlsson**

Surely men also suffer from these self-doubts, I hear you say. Of course they do, just not to the same degree.

According to the US National Bureau of Economic Research 'working paper', The Gender Gap in Self Promotion (2019), women consistently rated their performance as lower than men's, even though both groups had the same average score. Where men, on average, gave themselves 61 out of 100, women gave themselves 46. Even when told that an employer would use their self-evaluation to decide whether to hire them and what to pay them, women still self-promoted less than men.[75]

When Peta Credlin and I discuss the defining factors in how men and women approach workplace opportunities, her observations echo the research. She said when she was on the staffing committee, 'the women were too tough on their own performance and didn't seem to have a very good line of sight, whereas a bloke will upsell himself.' She elaborated, 'If a job advert in politics or a seat becomes vacant, the guy will look down the list and go, "can't do that, can't do that, can't do that, can do that, yep, I'll apply." Then the women will say, "I can do that, yes, I can do that" and then they get to the bottom, and they can't do the last thing and will go, "well I can't apply because I can't do all 10." It's never a question for the men though.'

It seems the studies back it up. The National Bureau of Economic Research show 80 per cent of women struggle with low self-esteem and shy away from self-advocacy at work.[76] It starts as soon as we step foot in the workplace and early on in our careers. A study of graduating MBA students found that half the men had negotiated their job offers compared to only one-eighth of the women.[77]

For confidence levels at work, men take the cake. By the age of 42, men are 34 per cent more likely to be in the top jobs than women, 'with overconfidence explaining 11 per cent of the gender gap'.[78] Factor in being a working mother, and systemic barriers become the biggest hurdle. Studies by the Centre for Longitudinal Studies at the University College London found factors related to family, employment conditions and societal norms contribute greatly to holding working mothers back from entering the top jobs.[79]

A lifetime of exposure to even subtle, unintended discrimination takes its toll. Being underestimated is just one part of the equation. Examining the cumulative effect of these factors, we can't be surprised when women's lack of self-belief is so insistent on and resistant to change.

During my interview with Julia Ross, we talked about adversity. Julia reminded me that the real challenge is not what happens to us but how we respond.

Julia Ross: 'Failing wasn't an option'

When Julia talked about perseverance, resilience and adversity, her determination was evident. She shared how, despite immense challenges, she never doubted her ability to succeed.

Julia recounted, 'In my career, I never doubted my ability to survive. I mean, when I first started off on my own and opened Julia Ross Personnel, it was far from ideal. Basically, I had an argument with my boss. I resigned, put my keys down and realised it was the keys to the house, the car, my job, everything.'

'It was traumatic at the time to be in a foreign country having no job, no house, no car and then realising you were pregnant. I sold everything I owned to raise enough money to start the business. So, yes, adversity drove my

(continued)

> need for success. It drove me much harder. There was no chance of failing. It wasn't an option.'
>
> She continued by sharing with me an instance where her bank manager requested her business figures. 'I need your figures,' he told her. When she questioned why, he replied, 'Well, we have a responsibility to make sure you don't lose your own money.'
>
> Julia's response: 'Well, I think we'll leave that to me, won't we?' She recounted, 'We banked with them, but we didn't have a loan.' They didn't get her figures until the company went public, a subtle assertion of control over her own destiny.
>
> Her reflections on how gender played a role in these experiences are particularly striking. 'I don't believe he would have done that had I been a male. That stuff was evident from day one, really. And it's been evident all the way through my career. So, it's what you do about it that's the difference.'
>
> 'Go around these obstacles, manoeuvre yourself around them. Sometimes, you can't waste time and energy fighting it directly. It's a smarter way to go about it.'

Carrying the burden of bias to the workforce

Think about the stories I shared in chapter 2 of this book: Sam, the Shortboard Surfer, the Girl in the Sauna, and Sara, whose mother 'hopes she marries well'. These are case studies of discrimination, gender bias and underestimation. But as recitals go, they are ordinary.

They aren't big-news stories designed to provoke outrage. They don't feature instances of violent oppression or outrageous sexism. They are subtle—and that's the point. Most likely, these accounts feel very familiar. Undoubtedly you could tell me many similar tales off the top of your head. These are the insidious, subtle events that occur thousands of times in every woman's life. And they are from the here and now.

The ages of the young women in the stories vary from 23 to 33 years. How do they successfully navigate the work arena, compete for a role, put their hand up to be seen, or take on a promotion or advancement, let alone compete in a male-dominated industry when burdened with gender self-doubt baggage and (often) fragile self-esteem?

Here is the real kicker: these young women won't even know they are carrying it. Snuck into the periphery—burrowed in tick-like—it's barely noticeable. Attributed to years of subtle, gentle, even ingrained gender bias, they won't realise it, applying for roles with passivity instead of assertiveness, hesitation instead of enthusiasm ... and the pattern continues.

They are young, not even remotely exposed to the toxicity and damage ongoing bias brings. That's if they let it. Even with heightened awareness, it is a guarantee they will take some of the legacy with them as they have families and raise daughters—and that's why the estimate to closing the gap is 257 years.

Until women better leverage workplace opportunities, according to my calculations, they can count on experiencing at least $1 million in lost earnings and more than $100 000 in lost superannuation benefits. For clarity, these estimations are not based on having to have a career or high-earning jobs. They are determined by the decisions you make.

I acknowledge the enormous challenge in combatting the accumulated years of bias, discrimination and being underestimated. I recognise how the outer world shapes the inner, forming the mind's negative life scripts and limiting self-beliefs. You can't just turn your back on these and be a new you.

Or can you? Kristina Karlsson, a self-described serial entrepreneur, thinks you can. She says, 'My kind of view on life is you can't change other people. You can only change yourself.'

Kristina's business, Dream Life, is about making your dreams a reality, so I think she might know a thing or two about changing your script, mindset and life's outcome.

> *I'm a serial entrepreneur. I keep getting up again. I had an attitude of knowing anything is possible.*
> **Kristina Karlsson**

It's not going to be easy. Of course, it will be a challenge. But it can be done, and it should be done! It starts with small, incremental, yet brave and meaningful decisions. Just before we get to these new and more powerful decisions, let's take a short detour to discuss hard work and resilience ... they are necessary ingredients to assist you with this challenge.

Hard work and resilience

The moment we are told something is hard work, it seems it is an auto body recoil. There is nothing attractive or remotely glamorous about the concept of hard work—even the words themselves are short and sharp, almost barked out as an order. No-one in the history of life ever said, 'Please, if there is one thing I want the most from my life, it is for it to be hard work.'

Yet, while society recoils at the mention of hard work, it remains a cornerstone of real achievement. The women I interviewed—Julia Ross, Leila McKinnon, Nagi Maehashi, Kristina Karlsson, Peta Credlin and Professor Fiona Wood—had many things in common. Yet, the main message that came through was the importance of hard work and the part it played in their lives and success.

Now I know what you might be thinking. Am I trying to say that women don't work hard? Of course not. I'm not talking about the hard work of labour, both domestic and professional. Women have that well and truly covered. I'm talking about the hard work of standing up for yourself, again and again, even when it's uncomfortable, and pushing through.

> *Hard work... there is no substitute for it. Nothing is going to land in your lap.*
> **Peta Credlin**

Hard work doesn't have to mean long hours. Paraphrasing the interviews, it's about working through the challenging times, keeping focused on the goal and not giving up on yourself. The 'hard' part is not in the doing. It's not your boss asking you to work 6 days a week or pull a 12-hour shift every day for a week. In comparison, that would be easy.

Fiona Wood recalls, 'I had to be a bit more forceful in proving myself in those days. I worked hard because that's what I do. I just kept going.'

The 'hard' in hard work is the mental and emotional toughness to get through. This is why resilience was the other factor that was abundantly apparent in each of these interviews.

What is resilience, really?

'Resilience is the process and outcome of successfully adapting to difficult or challenging life experiences, especially through mental, emotional and behavioural flexibility and adjustment to external and internal demands.'[80] The good news is resilience can be cultivated and developed.

In conversation with Fiona Wood for this book, we spoke about resilience as a necessary and all-important life skill. She described it as 'a learned behaviour'. Fiona believes we should all invest in resilience:

> *The smart money is to invest in your resilience. You can't predict when you will be under the pump and need it, and you will need it at some point.*

Along with the incredible women I interviewed, I also met with a highly accomplished man. I spoke with Phil Kearns, a former Australian rugby union player, captain for the Wallabies and CEO of AV Jennings. He had similar comments about the importance of resilience.

Phil Kearns: 'Be prepared for rejection — it won't kill you'

Being heavily involved with athletes, both men and women, Phil says the 'capacity for resilience is a fundamental skill and when carried through to the workplace plays out as a true advantage'.

If you are unsure how resilience can be learned, Phil provides a simple yet insightful observation of building resilience, perseverance and courage at a young age. Phil reflects on the use of social media — the way we communicate so freely via text as opposed to by phone or face-to-face — and compares it to his time as a teenager.

'There were no mobile phones. If you wanted to ring up a girl for a date, first you had to get her number. You can go to her direct or through her friends: possible rejection number one.

'So, you get the number and some courage to call, but all along you think, "Shit, is her dad going to answer?" More trepidation, fear and possible rejection number two.

'Then you have to get through the conversation with the dad or mum, if you're lucky. But then, what if she doesn't want to speak with you? More courage is needed and possible rejection number three.

'It's either yes or no. Either way, you are not going to die, so go for it!'

Phil and others have made the point that building resilience often comes from exposing yourself to uncomfortable situations again and again until they become easier. They don't have to be huge, anxiety-provoking events. The regular, incremental effort is what matters. Slowly, over time, those efforts add up.

Phil comments, 'As a teenager developing my understanding of the social world, the whole way along, I was building some courage and resilience, but I didn't think it as that at the time. However, now, with easy use of texts and messaging, emojis dismantle some of those micro-opportunities to build these necessary personal and professional skills.'

It is a simple example showing how small daily moments of being in an uncomfortable zone can build resilience.

Don't wait until the big-ticket disaster or challenge comes in. It might be too late. Being ill-prepared and not having enough invested resilience from previous experiences could be the cause of the 'devastation' as opposed to the challenge at hand. Without enough resilience, you might not cope at all.

> *I worked my guts out from day one and I loved it. I want to do well. I just pick myself up and dust myself off and I keep going.*
> **Nagi Maehashi**

You wouldn't do a marathon if you had never gone for a run in your life. You need practice to build up to the main event. You might start with a 3-kilometre run and find it tough. The next time you do it, you at least know what to expect and prepare yourself. To run the marathon, you need smaller preparational runs!

Resilience for the big ticket-times is similar. Face some of life's tough challenges to keep building resilience and that necessary bounce-back factor. It's not just about getting through a difficult time. It's how you get through. Think of it as an investment, as Fiona does. Gradually bank the experiences of resilience and difficult times. Create a resilience savings plan.

Here are some pointers to help you build resilience:

- *Learn from mistakes and challenges.* Use setbacks and 'failures' as learning opportunities for next time. 'Ah, last time I didn't spend enough time preparing that report, and that's why I couldn't articulate it well in the meeting. Now I know I need 5 days to prep.'

- *Ask for help.* You don't have to 'get through' it on your own. Learning to seek support is also a valuable lesson in resilience.

- *Change the narrative.* Saying you can't do something will inevitably mean, 'you can't do something'. Turn it into 'How will I do this?' Kristina Karlsson proffers this advice even when she gets a 'no' for an idea or business venture. She says she shares it with her team and even her children so they can experience the minor setback, and then she tries to turn it around or pivot.

- *Don't shy away from difficult or uncomfortable situations.* Have faith that by applying effort you will get through it. Embrace it as a learning experience.

- *Seek out opportunities to grow.* Consider saying yes before saying no. Mention to your boss that you are up for a challenge!

Making small, incremental, yet brave and meaningful decisions to close the pay gap

You can wait for the societal shift and structural changes to take effect. But they won't happen in your lifetime. Or you can take a different route and bring about change for yourself to close the pay gap. Nothing dramatic, but mostly certainly empowering. The starting point and cornerstone is making small, incremental, yet brave and meaningful decisions.

Let's step through this powerful strategy:

- *Small:* The decisions don't have to be big. They can be incidental and even be the ones you make daily. They can be as basic as deciding to step forward and contribute at the next meeting — if your habit, like mine when studying with a class full of males, was to shrink into the background. Prepare beforehand so you don't let self-sabotage trip you up! That's its job. Self-sabotage loves to reinforce self-limiting beliefs!

- *Incremental:* Then you do it again at the next meeting, or the next appropriate opportunity to be seen and heard. One good decision builds and leads to even better decisions, increasing your confidence, self-esteem and abilities. It could be the impetus to secure a better role in the future. Keep using preparation and practice as your allies. They are bravery's fuel, helping the decisions you make to be successful ones.

- *Brave:* Whether you're a mountain climber, an adventure sports enthusiast or engaged in any activity that requires courage, preparation assumes and mitigates risk. Your perceived risk could be the fear of looking foolish or stumbling over your words in a presentation. Preparation can even involve practising out loud what you want to say. You may well be out of your comfort zone at times and will question yourself, be worried and revert to self-doubt. That's part of being brave.

- *Meaningful:* Decisions must be considered, not merely habitual. If your previous choices were shaped by fear of failure, avoiding new roles or challenges, then it's time to reassess.

Make each decision count, and make them active, not rudimentary, cursory or passive. Understand consequences, and, if possible, strip away the comforting illusions we often cling to. That part is difficult, I know! For example, extending maternity leave might feel like the right choice at the moment, but it warrants deeper reflection. The heart may pull in one direction, but the long-term financial and career impact deserves thoughtful consideration.

When well considered, you have decided the benefits outweigh the costs. You will have calculated the lost earnings for that additional time off and, if paying off a mortgage or saving for a deposit, also contemplated the impact. Perhaps you are looking at additional skills training to counter possible career stagnation. Ultimately, meaningful, well-thought-out decisions can equate to a sense of empowerment instead of feeling lost or ambling, which is sometimes the case.

Here are some decisions you can make:

- Ask for or accept training and learning opportunities.

- Negotiate better terms.

- Ask for salary increases.

- Ask for help at work.

- Ask for help at home.

- Seek out mentorship proactively.

- Replace 'I can't' with 'How can I?' to open up possibilities.

- Be discerning in choosing tasks that align with your goals.

- Master the art of saying 'no' and 'yes' thoughtfully and purposefully.

The $1 million can be yours by using the cumulative and compound effect of women making small, incremental, yet brave and meaningful decisions as they go through life. The cumulative effect of your better and stronger decision making transfers to your earnings, which equally enjoy the benefit of compound growth over your lifetime.

The inconvenience of having to work

'I wish I didn't have to go to work!'

Don't worry if you think this occasionally. You are not alone. We all do at times. However, as someone who lives and breathes all aspects of employment, I have to raise the topic of your relationship with your job ... it can make the difference to your earning potential.

Sometimes, we think of work as an annoying adjunct to life, a necessary evil, instead of it being welcomed in as a pivotal part of life. Our jobs are the vehicle for purpose, personal growth, relationships, learning, development and, of course, for our financial wellbeing. They provide the resources we need to pursue our dreams and support those we love.

Consider the trajectory of our lives: we go to preschool, then move through school, the educational and learning ground where children gain basic knowledge and social interaction. Some of us continue to university or other studies: the further education and learning that help us as we enter early adulthood.

Ultimately, most of us end up employed. The workforce is the next level and stage of our learning, development and growth—that's my view as an employment expert. We don't just enter the workforce and remain static. I'm not just referring to technical skills.

In fact, I mostly refer to the human behavioural aspects and the elements we can learn about ourselves. Leverage the opportunity for human and self-insight and, in doing so, perhaps consider your job as not only the key to achieving life's necessities but also to unlocking your aspirations. Instead of an irksome inconvenience, our jobs can be the catalyst for life-defining adventures.

> *I was seeking an adventure. I'm good at backing myself and being a bit bullish and charging at things. I was very ambitious.*
> **Leila McKinnon**

When we put more thought into 'what's for lunch' than workplace decisions

We carefully choose our partners and friends, where to live and whether to save for a house deposit. Yet, when we see our job as merely 'extra' to life rather than a fundamental part of it we fail to apply the same level of thoughtful decision making as we do to other major life choices. I see this all too frequently.

People often quit their jobs as an emotional reaction, without fully considering the consequences. I am not just talking about the short-term financial impact. I am referring to reputational risks, the ability to secure positive references for future opportunities, off the record remarks that could circulate and the challenge of explaining the decision to quit. And, of course, there's more.

Sometimes, and this is no exaggeration, people will put more thought into what they are having for lunch than into the impulse decision to quit their job. A $10 lunch versus a million-dollar career decision.

Just as we carefully weigh options for education, housing, relationships, family planning and travel, we should approach our work with equal deliberation.

The following is an example of the typical life transaction of paying off a mortgage, presenting considerations and decisions that we can equally apply to our workplace. Those small, incremental, yet brave and meaningful decisions.

Paying off the mortgage

Consider your accountant or bank manager advising you to pay an extra $100 a week off your mortgage. Or maybe it's your credit card that needs to be paid off. You nearly choke when they say it, slumping in the chair in a mock adult tantrum. It's half denial because you know what they are saying is correct. Yet, you can't help but think, 'It is easy for them, they aren't in my shoes!'

The better and braver decision is to make the extra repayments, which will go a long way to providing financial security and stability. It's tough at the time, especially in the beginning when you are already struggling to meet the existing repayments. But you know deep down, the advice is right. You don't need that trip to Mecca anyway! Ultimately, it's your choice, though.

The better, braver and more mindful workplace decisions we make to be financially ahead also seem arduous at the time. They challenge our mind script, beliefs and the rhetoric we tell ourselves, family, friends and colleagues. We want to reject and refute them with a whole lot more impetus than a tantrum. After all, the job is an annoying adjunct to life!

Trust me, just like that first extra $100 payment, the micro shifts in your decision making are the starting points. They form the foundation for future actions, behaviours and decisions to make that $1 million over your lifetime, yours. Apply for the promotion, even if you do not meet all the qualifications, experience or skills. It might just see you land the role. Or, as consolation, perhaps your manager puts you on a course to upskill. At the very worst, you gain experience for next time, when you will nail the interview and the job!

Your mindset should be, *Even if I don't get the job, I'm already ahead by going through the experience*. Leila McKinnon provides great insight on this point. She says from her experience, 'women often overthink, when we should just put our hand up and go for it'. Her advice is to 'watch men and how they back themselves'. She goes on to say, admirably, of former New Zealand Prime Minister Jacinda Ardern, 'I asked what her advice would be for young women, and it was exactly that: "Get the job and then work out how you are going to do it because you are never going to think you're perfect enough for the opportunity at the time."'

Julia Ross had a similar approach when taking on an overly daunting challenge. 'We are going to do this, chew like hell and just make it happen. And we always did make it happen. It was a matter of committing and setting your mind to it.' I can tell you from personal experience, the most wonderful part of working with a courageous female leader like Julia is that you go along for the ride. 'I had no fear of taking anyone into anything with me either.' And she didn't!

> *The difference is, at your core, do you believe the advice to change the way you have been making decisions about your job is right? Or will you continue on the same path?*

Forming habits

As advised by your accountant, you start to pay the extra $100 a week onto your mortgage, and get accustomed to it. It becomes part of the pattern and the way you live. Occasionally, it's frustrating, even demoralising, when you're tempted by a holiday — the one all your friends are begging you to join them on. Or you see some new furniture when the sales are on (and your sofa is older than God) or toys and gadgets the children nag you for because 'all their friends have them'. And what about those house renovations?

The list goes on. There is always something to entice and woo us. It's hard and a part of the challenge when working towards achieving the goals we deem important to us. It's no different as we go along in our jobs and at work.

On occasion, there are temptations to revert to the old mindset of how you used to handle a workplace scenario, picking the path that seems easier — 'better for us' on the surface — but really, it's not. For example, accepting a 2.5 per cent salary increase and saying nothing when you were expecting 4 per cent. Or knowing you need opportunities to be 'seen' at work but saying 'no' when asked to present to a room of 300 people.

Over time, as the habit forms, it becomes easier. Just like making the repayments, the new way of seeing yourself and making those brave and mindful decisions at work seems run of the mill. Habits often become second nature, leading us to perform them automatically. Not noticing the 'struggle' so much, they become the way of life.

To the point where, seeing the benefits, you increase your extra repayments to $200 and the loan starts to come down exponentially. It's the same as at work. You have more confidence in handling matters that previously would have deterred you. You volunteer for the presentations, and instead of waiting for a salary review, you pre-empt the salary increase discussion, asking for 5.5 per cent instead of the 4 per cent they were expecting to give you. It feels good.

It's worth it when you are mortgage-free 7 years plus ahead of time. It's liberating. If only you'd added extra repayments sooner! So, too, when you are unshackled from internal constraints to be your authentic self at work, ask for what you want, strive for more, and have belief in your potential and abilities to earn what you deserve. If only you had made those small, incremental, yet brave and meaningful decisions earlier!

The advice from the accountant, the benefits, the pain and discomfort of following the suggestions, and the mind's game in throwing doubt and suspicion on the advice to lure you away from the ultimate goal are oddly similar to our workplace dynamics.

So here's your to-do list:

- Apply for the promotion, even if you think you don't have all the qualifications.

- Ask for a salary increase if you feel you deserve it. Pre-empt the salary increase conversation and speak up if you expected more remuneration for your work.

- Say 'yes' when asked to present to a group of people or any other learning opportunity, even, and especially if, it puts you in the 'uncomfortable zone'.

Better still...

- Volunteer for the presentation.

- Take the promotion your boss puts you forward for and then do what Leila McKinnon, Peta Credlin and Julia Ross do: work out how to do it afterwards. Back yourself, commit and work hard.

- Say 'yes' to training, upskilling and learning opportunities. You don't know where they will take you.

- Participate in virtual or face-to-face meetings and be seen and heard.

- If you have a good idea or differing opinion, find your voice and express it.

These are just some of the small and different decisions to make. They only scratch the surface. There are a million, just like the dollars: micro-decisions we make every day that can effect change. A million dollars worth of change.

We attribute considerable responsibility for the gender pay gap to external authorities, society, institutions, organisations and structures—as we duly should. However, waiting for the changes to come through isn't an option. We'll be dead if we wait that long! Instead, let's overcome the internal forces—yes, the ones imposed on us through bias, discrimination and their entourage. Dismantle the constraints, empower ourselves and support one another. I believe our capacity to do so is immense.

I have an attitude
of knowing
anything is
possible. And
I also have an
attitude that I can
learn anything.

KRISTINA KARLSSON,
KIKKI.K

Chapter 5

THE MILLION-DOLLAR FORMULA

In this chapter, I talk about the power of incrementalism when it comes to building women's wealth. I show you how purposeful decision making—yes, those small, incremental yet brave decisions (from chapter 4)—leads to greater earning power. These seemingly minor decisions put women in a stronger earning position, setting in motion the compound effect of their earnings.

The power of compounding helps money grow faster. While it's a financial concept, it can also be applied to our decisions and actions. In consideration of the workplace, these better, smarter decisions become lifetime habits, compounding to provide lifelong benefits. A million dollars of benefits.

How to earn or lose your million dollars

Let's see how these different and courageous decisions effect the change we all desire.

Surprising facts: not surprising ... shocking

- Currently, women retire with $136 000 less in superannuation than men.

- Women in the top 20 per cent of income earners experience the largest gender pay gap.

- Women in the lowest 20 per cent income bracket are living 4.1 fewer years than the 20 per cent wealthiest.

- *Euro News* reported that only 43 per cent of women have asked for a pay rise during their careers, despite most feeling unsatisfied with their salaries.[81]

- According to the ABS, '31 per cent of retired women [rely] on their partner's income to meet their living costs at retirement'.[82]

Much like constantly tolerating gender discrimination can have an accumulative negative effect on our confidence and mindset, so too can workplace decisions have an accumulative positive or negative effect on our earnings.

Think of the compound effect of good decision making and earnings as planting a tree. The commitment of regular watering and caring for the tree equates to the mindful decisions we make. Each good decision builds on the last, leading to steady growth. Similarly, the compound effect of earnings is like the tree yielding fruit. As your earnings grow, they can generate more earnings through interest, investments or reinvestment. Over time, both your good decisions and growth in earnings work together to create a much larger and healthier 'tree'. This process, known as compounding, means that small, consistent positive actions and earnings can lead to significant long-term growth and success.

Of course, we don't always make good decisions. That's also normal and fine. What truly matters is our ability to recognise our choices, the direction they've set us on, and the course of action required to move forward. For example, forgetting to feed or water the tree might see you miss out on that season's fruit, leading to a different course of action. Now the tree requires a super fertiliser, a prune or perhaps a severe cutback to bring it back to luscious fruiting again. It's all part of the real-life journey of learning and growing. It's never, ever perfect (or easy, for that matter)!

The compound effect on earnings

In this section I model five different everyday financial scenarios to show you, on a basic level, the various compound effects on earnings. These scenarios are 'real life' and show the situations women often find themselves in and the approaches and decisions they make. For ease of demonstrating, I might refer to 'salary increases'. These are not necessarily increases for doing the same job. They could be salary increases due to having changed jobs, receiving a promotion or taking up a better opportunity. Basically, asking for more. More acknowledgement, accolades, appreciation, promotions or opportunities to be heard. The point is to demonstrate the cumulative impact of even seemingly small salary increases through better decision making: the kind you might not think are a big deal or worth going after.

For simplicity, I've used the following numbers for all scenarios and examples:

- statistics from the ABS. The full-time seasonally adjusted adult average weekly wage is $1888.80.[83] As an annual equivalent, this equates to $98 217.60 (rounded off to $98 217)

- statistics for wage growth from the Australian Industry Group, using the long-run average yearly wage growth of 2.4 per cent.[84] I should mention, wage growth relates to the consumer price index (CPI) or inflation. Additionally, not all organisations apply this. It is not legislated and is entirely at the discretion of the employer

Note: I have deliberately used pre-COVID figures to allow for standard inflation. I haven't used post-COVID data as these figures show that wages increased by over 4 per cent. For what I am trying to demonstrate, conservative, long-run statistics are realistic and don't inflate the outcome.

SCENARIO 1: NOT RECEIVING A SALARY INCREASE FOR 10 YEARS... AND NOT ASKING FOR ONE

Some of you reading this might think I'm exaggerating to make a point. I wish I was, but this really happens—and often! It is most certainly the situation for many women. In fact, I have met candidates who have had more than 10 years between salary increases. Many women reading this will be nodding knowingly and silently. It isn't something we admit to our friends or colleagues. Maybe that's part of the issue. Much like the emperor from the fable in chapter 4, perhaps we don't want to face reality. Well, take a look at table 5.1 for some realism.

Table 5.1: no salary increase for 10 years

Scenario 1	Salary remaining at $98 217	Salary of $98 217 + 2.4% wage growth	Increase amount
Year 1	$98 217	$100 574	$2 357
Year 2	$98 217	$102 988	$4 771
Year 3	$98 217	$105 460	$7 243
Year 4	$98 217	$107 991	$9 774
Year 5	$98 217	$110 583	$12 366
Year 6	$98 217	$113 237	$15 020
Year 7	$98 217	$115 955	$17 738
Year 8	$98 217	$118 738	$20 521
Year 9	$98 217	$121 588	$23 371
Year 10	$98 217	$124 506	$26 289
Total increase			**$139 450**

The modelling in table 5.1 clearly reflects the financial impact of not receiving even the minimum wage growth. At the end of the 10-year period, the woman in scenario 1 is earning $98 217 compared to $124 506 if the minimum wage growth had been applied. That's an annual salary difference of $26 289. Wait for it though ... The grand total in lost earnings over 10 years is $139 450. I know, it makes me wince too. What could you or your family have done with the extra money? A lot!

There are two factors at play here:

- the place where you work not providing increases over the years (10 years)

- you not asking for an increase.

Often, when faced with the situation of not receiving a pay rise, we write it off and say it's okay. The justification being, 'It's only $2357. I mean, after tax, it's not that much and not worth the angst of having the discussion with my boss.' Hmm ...

Perhaps you might even think, over a 10-year period, 'It's only $23 570' (10 years × $2357). Well, this modelling proves it's not just $2357 per year. The difference in earnings is a staggering $139 450.

The more time goes by, the more powerful compounding becomes. By not speaking up over the 10-year period, not only have you missed out on getting ahead financially, but you have also gone backwards in your earnings. Let me explain.

The dollar value of money—allowing for inflation—means your $98 217 was worth more 10 years ago, which means you could buy more with it back then than today.

Using the Reserve Bank Australia's tool for the dollar value of money[85], $100 at the supermarket in 2009 would have been the equivalent of $123.29 in 2019. If you are the person in scenario 1, to have the same purchasing power you had in 2009 on a salary of $98 217, you need to be earning $121 095 in 2019 just to keep up with inflation.

> *My question to the women in scenario 1 is, why don't you speak up? It's a rhetorical question because, of course, we know why. Here is an uncomfortable truth: the longer you wait to voice your worth, the more daunting it becomes. Growing heavier with time, weighing on both mind and resolve, it too has a compound effect, but with a bleak outcome. Know, though, you are not alone.*

I must be frank though, because I don't want to set people up for crushing conversations. Organisations often withhold pay rises as a way of communicating that performance is not up to standard. I don't agree with this passive communication or management style, but disappointingly, it's quite normal. What if this is the case for you, and your boss thinks your performance isn't at the level required?

Don't be the emperor, settling for denial. It's far better to be brave and ask for a meeting to discuss a pay rise and possibly your performance. Isn't it better that you know the truth? If the answer is that your performance is below par, ask what you can do to improve. As difficult as it might be, it can be empowering. You get to decide if what they are saying has merit. If yes, then take it on board, improve and earn the increases sooner. If no, then you get to decide whether to leave and earn more, or stay. Surely, if it's 'no', you leave? Again, be brave.

Scenario 1 only demonstrates the difference if an increase was aligned with the minimum wage growth. We are not even talking about the wage increases attributed to performance. If you want to know what that figure would be, look at scenario 2.

SCENARIO 2: RECEIVING A 5 PER CENT SALARY INCREASE EVERY 3 YEARS WITH 2.4 PER CENT WAGE GROWTH IN-BETWEEN

Let's look at a woman who receives a salary increase due to good performance (conservatively at 5 per cent) every 3 years and applying 2.4 per cent minimum wage growth in the years in-between. As table 5.2 (overleaf) illustrates, this is a seemingly modest rate of increase.

Table 5.2: salary increases of 5 per cent every 3 years and 2.4 per cent in the in-between years

Scenario 2	Salary of $98 217 + 5% increase every 3 years* and 2.4% wage growth in between	Increase amount
Year 1	$103 128	$4 911
Year 2	$105 603	$7 386
Year 3	$108 137	$9 920
Year 4	$113 544	$15 327
Year 5	$116 269	$18 052
Year 6	$119 059	$20 842
Year 7	$125 012	$26 795
Year 8	$128 012	$29 795
Year 9	$131 084	$32 867
Year 10	$137 638	$39 421
10-year total		**$205 316**

* Years 1, 4, 7 and 10

Yet it represents a monumental difference in earnings over a 10-year period, just from receiving performance-based salary increases. You can see the significance of the compound and accelerated growth.

In scenario 1, with no increases at all, the difference in salary after 10 years is $98 217 versus $124 506 (with minimum wage growth increases). Compare that to a difference of $137 638 in scenario 2. The person in scenario 2 earns a difference in annual salary of $39 421, and over the 10-year period, the total difference is $205 316 (or $65 866 if minimum wage growth of 2.4 per cent was applied as per scenario 1). What about when its performance review time? You are expecting at least a 5 per cent increase in salary, but your boss comes back with 2.5 per cent. You accept it and say nothing.

SCENARIO 3: ACCEPTING A 2.5 PER CENT SALARY INCREASE WHEN EXPECTING 5 PER CENT, WITH 2.4 PER CENT WAGE GROWTH THEREAFTER

What about scenario 3 (table 5.3), where you are expecting a 5 per cent salary increase and instead accept a 2.5 per cent increase and receive only 2.4 per cent wage growth thereafter over a 5-year period?

By accepting the 2.5 per cent increase instead of negotiating harder and asking for 5 per cent, the difference in earnings over the 5-year period is $12884. You might reason that the difference in the first year between the 2.5 per cent increase and the 5 per cent increase is only $2456 — but again, consider the bigger picture and compound effect over time.

Table 5.3: accepting a 2.5 per cent salary increase when expecting it to be 5 per cent

Scenario 3	Salary of $98 217 + 2.5% increase and 2.4% wage growth thereafter	Salary of $98 217 + 5% increase and 2.4% wage growth thereafter	Difference in earnings
Year 1	$100 672	$103 128	$2456
Year 2	$103 088	$105 603	$2515
Year 3	$105 562	$108 137	$2575
Year 4	$108 095	$110 732	$2637
Year 5	$110 689	$113 390	$2701
5-year total			**$12 884**

SCENARIO 4: ASKING FOR A 7 PER CENT SALARY INCREASE AND GETTING IT, WITH 2.4 PER CENT WAGE GROWTH THEREAFTER

What about being brave and asking for a 7 per cent increase — because you have done your research and believe that's your worth (instead of 2.5 per cent)? That's what scenario 4 in table 5.4 (overleaf) examines.

Scenario 4 shows a difference in earnings of $23 189 by receiving a 7 per cent increase rather than settling for 2.5 per cent. Over 5 years, $23 189 is a substantial figure, let alone what that equates to over a lifetime of compounding. All by showing initiative, being brave and taking your financial future into your own hands.

Table 5.4: being brave — asking for a 7 per cent salary increase

Scenario 4	Salary of $98 217 + 7% increase and 2.4% wage growth thereafter	Salary of $98 217 + 2.5% increase and 2.4% wage growth thereafter	Difference in earnings	Difference in earnings if salary remains at $98 217
Year 1	$105 092	$100 672	$4 420	$6 875
Year 2	$107 614	$103 088	$4 526	$9 397
Year 3	$110 197	$105 562	$4 635	$11 980
Year 4	$112 842	$108 095	$4 747	$14 625
Year 5	$115 550	$110 689	$4 861	$17 333
5-year total			**$23 189**	**$60 210**

Often, we go along with the decision proffered to us. Do not be fooled: these are not our decisions; these are our acquiesces. There is a difference.

You may need to ask yourself: What is the worst that could happen if I ask for a pay rise? That you won't receive the increase, and you will just be in the same position? If you don't ask, you will remain in the same situation anyway. At least by asking, even if it is a no, it's on your boss's mind and 'agenda' for next time, which is powerful. The decision to ask is a small, incremental step in the right direction. Not to mention a brave and meaningful one!

Handling the discussion the right way is key to negating any backlash — if that is what you are concerned about. But here is a question worth pondering, would a man worry about that? I'm not so sure.

When I spoke to Nagi Maehashi about pay increases, she gave the exact same advice: 'It is all about how you ask for it.' As long as you do it the right way, professionally and be yourself, what have you got to lose?'

If it helps to provide you with a bit more courage, Nagi also said to me, 'I was in the corporate world long enough to observe that men are more aggressive about pay rises and promotions. It's the truth. I also fully recognise what I am saying is a stereotype, but it is what I saw.'

Scenario 4 also demonstrates the difference in earnings compared to scenario 1, with no salary increase. The difference in earnings over 5 years is $60 210.

These are not figures we can easily ignore. They are our reality, though. Situations such as scenarios 3 and 4 might be when you are negotiating the salary for a new job, which is a critical time to assert your worth.

These four scenarios are simple everyday situations. By making different and better decisions—small, yet brave and meaningful ones—we create incremental adjustments and changes to our immediate earnings, with significant contributions over our lifetime.

To begin your personal mission to close the million-dollar gap, you don't have to have a high-flying career or copious amounts of overtime work. Instead, start by focusing on making decisions that put you in the position to earn more and don't be afraid to ask for the compensation you believe you deserve with strong self-advocacy and confidence.

SCENARIO 5: BEING OFFERED A PROMOTION AND A $10 000 SALARY INCREASE ... AND SAYING NO

Scenario 4 deals with being comfortable asking for what we deserve. However, bridging the million-dollar gap requires more than just pay rises and minimum wage growth: it needs women to put themselves in positions of growth, opportunity and empowerment. Let us take it up a notch.

Your boss offers you a promotion, and it comes with a $10 000 pay increase. You are flattered, nervously excited even. Then the self-doubt kicks in. You worry that you are not capable, that you are not experienced or skilled enough. You know it would be great for your career and growth, but you thought an opportunity like this would be at least 2 years away. You say no. See table 5.5 (overleaf) for details on what you've just sacrificed.

Table 5.5: saying no to a $10 000 salary increase

Scenario 5	Salary of $98 217 + $10 000 increase, then 2.4% wage growth	Salary of $98 217 + 2.4% wage growth	Difference in earnings
Year 1	$108 217	$100 574	$7 643
Year 2	$110 814	$102 988	$7 826
Year 3	$113 474	$105 460	$8 014
Year 4	$116 197	$107 991	$8 206
Year 5	$118 986	$110 583	$8 403
5-year total			**$40 092**

You are not missing out on $10 000: over 5 years, it adds up to $40 092. And that's if your boss gives you the minimum wage growth each year. If they don't? Well, the loss in earnings over 5 years turns out to be over $70 000. Well, it's $76 603 to be exact. Five years goes by quickly and a lot can be done with an extra $70 000.

Opportunities like this can be daunting. Unfortunately, in pivotal moments you can expect self-doubt and the fear of failure to make an appearance. These unwelcome guests whisper and conspire. The negative narrative might convince you, 'I am not good enough' and you retreat from the challenge. It feels safer that way.

You justify that you do not need the $10 000 increase. This is where you pull out all stops, convincing yourself (falsely) that what you are doing is right, and *I'll take up the opportunity next time.* (What if there is no next time?) This rationalisation provides temporary comfort but, deep down, perpetuates a cycle of missed chances and unfulfilled potential.

It is important to understand which kind of psychological elements might play a role when it comes to your decision making. Not all that we do is conscious or rational. While unconscious biases often drive our emotions, they are just one piece of the puzzle. Our habits, instincts and ingrained patterns also play a role. By naming and recognising these forces, biases included, we begin to break the cycle of missing opportunities. By eliminating these traps that corrupt our rational minds, we see more clearly the decisions that are better for us, our potential and long-term goals.

We are versatile in creating stories that match our beliefs because facing reality means recognising uncomfortable truths. If we admit to being fearful, apathetic and lacking commitment, then we have no other option than to re-evaluate how we see ourselves. This kind of mental conflict would lead to deeper self-analysis and the beginning of questioning other beliefs we hold about ourselves.

But our minds often avoid difficult truths by creating stories that shield us from the discomfort of self-reflection. Going through such a process is often painful and uncomfortable, and the result is change. Change challenges our comfort zones, forcing us to confront fears and uncertainties, and we are not always great at that.

Whilst I say all of the above to encourage women to question the decisions that sometimes hold them back, it's important to remember that not every opportunity such as a promotion needs to be taken. Just make the decisions for the right reasons, not the ones that may cost you further. Being scared is normal, as is fearing failure, but don't let it hold you back — instead, channel it in a way that will help you find the road to success.

Nagi Maehashi provides a fabulous example of this when she sets out to start her own business, the one we all know well: RecipeTin Eats.

Nagi Maehashi: navigating the fear and not letting it hold you back

When I interviewed Nagi Maehashi, it was clear she is incredibly grounded and down to earth. Her stories, emotions, fears and feelings felt so relatable, they could be yours or mine.

Just before starting RecipeTin Eats, she told me how people thought she was 'crazy' and even asked her when she was coming back to 'the real world'. Nagi told me that she was scared — after all, she was leaving a full-time role with a great salary. However, she wasn't going to let that hold her back from achieving her dreams.

> Leaning in with her cheeky smile, Nagi confessed, 'I wasn't actually crazy. It was a well-thought-out and measured decision. I did my research and due diligence.' She explained how she conducted a SWOT analysis of her skills and abilities. For the record, Nagi didn't do the SWOT analysis to find reasons not to proceed with RecipeTin Eats. Instead, it was to figure out how to make it happen.
>
> The analyses highlighted the gaps, weaknesses and areas she needed to work on to improve, and pinpointed the skills she would need to be successful. As Nagi put it, 'You've got to be realistic and truthful with yourself.'
>
> (Later in the book, in chapter 9, I'll show you how to do your own SWOT analysis, just like Nagi did.)
>
> Before starting RecipeTin Eats, Nagi was a finance executive who had never held a camera in her life. Yet, all the photos on her socials, her website and even her books are taken by Nagi. She knew this was going to be a necessary skill and requirement for her success. She identified the gap and learned how to do it. 'I was honest with myself,' she told me. 'I knew I was going to need this skill, so I worked really hard at learning how to do it.'

The same applies to all of us. If there is an opportunity, especially when someone else is advocating for us and believing in our potential, we shouldn't let fear get in our way. Work out the skills gaps, create a plan to acquire them and seize the opportunity! Your workplace decision today has significant financial implications for the future.

Silvia's story: what would you do?

Here is another interesting, real–life scenario.

Silvia's boss believes in her abilities and potential and offers her an opportunity. It's a different role; however, it leverages her transferable skills and provides enormous earning potential, not to mention personal and professional growth. The important distinction in this story is that Silvia has her boss's complete backing, support and belief in her abilities. Does Silvia feel the same? Let's see …

Silvia is an office manager in a real estate firm, working 4 days a week and earning $100000 (pro rata to $80000 for 4 days). Silvia's husband works in a bank and earns $130000. They aspire to buy a house one day and maybe have a second child. They currently have a 2-year-old, and the balance of working 4 days works well for the family right now. Silvia plans to return to 5 days in the next year or so.

Silvia has been with the firm for 5 years, enjoys the job, likes the environment and her boss, but has received only three CPI increases over the 5 years, plus one $1000 bonus. There are 15 people in the team, and she takes care of everything, even HR and some accounts: she's a regular 'jack of all'. Silvia does a good job—she knows that because her boss tells her and so does the team.

The clients love dealing with Silvia. She knows them well and often manages simple transactions and queries for them. They even joke with her boss that they might 'poach her if he isn't careful'. Silvia has often thought about where to go from here.

Unexpectedly, Silvia's boss takes her out for lunch and offers her a 'promotion': would she like to become a sales agent? Her salary will increase immediately to $130000 and she will earn a commission as well. He says, 'You know the clients, the process and are practically doing the job anyway.' If she is serious about it, here is the plan:

- Silvia needs to work 5 days a week, not 4. When she becomes skilled, then there will be options for 4 days—like other experienced sales agents—but until she learns the craft, she must also invest in herself. But equally, the fifth day immediately means an additional $50000 (going from a salary of $80000 for 4 days to the promoted role with a salary increase to $130000 for 5 days).

- She needs to commit to the job and plan for 12 months so she can really experience the role. The company will hire a contractor to do her usual job during that period.

- After 12 months, if Silvia doesn't like the sales agent role, she can have her old job back.

There are moments in our careers when we're faced with decisions that seem straightforward but can have a big impact on our future. Do we go for the immediate financial boost and career advancement, or do we stick with what's working, where stability and work–life balance fit our family's needs at that moment? It's never an easy choice, and the trade-offs can feel daunting. Many women know this all too well. But these decisions often go beyond the here and now. What might seem like a small step today can have a ripple effect, shaping our future financial security.

In chapter 6, we will explore how these pivotal moments and decisions can impact our lifetime earnings and financial security. Understanding the long-term consequences of our choices is crucial.

Lifetime earnings: don't miss out on $1 million

Following are three example stories of women — Daisy, Masako and Paola — each making different decisions as they go through the course of their working life. They highlight the difference in lifetime earnings and the accumulation of superannuation. For simplicity and consistency, they have the same starting salaries, the same opportunities offered and no time off for caring responsibilities. The only variable is the decisions made. Additionally, these do not assume high career positions, as you'll see from the average salary I've used. These scenarios could be the future for Sam, the Shortboard Surfer, Smart Girl in the Sauna, Sara or you.

Note: for clarity and simplicity, the calculations do not consider the future value (FV) of money. As previously mentioned, the FV of money is the economic concept of the value of the current asset (dollar amount) at a future date based on assumed growth or, in this case, allowing for inflation.[86]

Here are the conservative assumptions I used when creating the example stories:

- average annual salary of $98 217
- annual wage growth of 2.4 per cent
- increase in salary if taking up a growth opportunity, promotion or advancement = 10 per cent (the calculation of 10 per cent every 5 years is conservative and from a low average wage growth in the interim 4-year period. Research shows companies typically offer top performers 2.5 times the amount offered to lower performers)[87]
- additional salary increases due to the progression path of accepting the initial opportunity estimated at every 5 years
- starting age of 38 years
- employer superannuation contribution of 12 per cent (effective 1 July 2025). Since the introduction of compulsory super in July 1992, the median growth fund has returned 7.9 per cent annually)[88]
- conservative super growth of 4 per cent
- for conservative calculations, 12 per cent superannuation is based on the contribution base (2024/25 maximum income per quarter for super guarantee purposes) of $65 070.

Daisy's story

Daisy is a high-performing employee. She is 38 years old and her annual salary is $98 217. Daisy is offered a promotion/ advancement and takes it. She receives an additional salary increase of 10 per cent of her total package every 5 years and in the years in between receives the standard 2.4 per cent wage growth.

The salary increase every 5 years is due to performance or additional career and job advancement. These come about through the compound positive effect of her proactive, as well as brave, decisions and choices at work. These decisions have increased her experience and learning even when she 'fails'.

Daisy says 'yes' to learning opportunities, puts her hand up, self-promotes and asks for salary increases. Make no mistake, Daisy still experiences ample self-doubt, loses confidence often, questions her abilities frequently and has bouts of anxiety. With awareness and deliberate actions, she chooses to work through them. However, as time progresses and these incrementally stronger decisions become habits (the compound effect of good habits), optimism and self-belief increase, and her confidence strengthens. All are building the path to better self-efficacy and earning power.

By making these decisions, at the age of 65 Daisy will have earned $1 298 040 more over her lifetime than Paola, and $912 265 more than Masako, whose stories follow.

When it comes to retirement and superannuation, Daisy will have accumulated $215 072 more than Paola and $137 282 more than Masako.

Even on a conservative salary, you can see that by making better decisions — somewhat career-based, but mostly growth-based decisions — the compound effect of her earnings could be up to $1 298 040 more over her lifetime.

Let's now read Masako's story.

Masako's story

Masako is also highly valued and a good performer. She is 38 years old and her annual salary is $98 217.

Masako accepts one promotion when it's first offered. But it's just the one. After that, she declines any further promotions and receives only the standard wage growth of 2.4 per cent for the rest of her working life. This could be due to not finding her purpose, not wanting to work on growth areas or simply being content with what she is doing.

In Masako's situation, circumstances could also be beyond her control. It might be a divorce, an illness, an injury, a diagnosis or a family member who is ill, and this means her attention is redirected elsewhere. We all know life doesn't always play out how we plan.

After making these decisions, at the age of 65 Masako will be $385775 ahead of Paola, but $912265 behind Daisy in lifetime earnings. As for her retirement, Masako will be $77790 ahead of Paola, and $137282 behind Daisy in accumulated superannuation.

Now let's turn our attention to Paola.

Paola's story

Paola is a hard worker and always does her best for her employers. She is 38 years old and her annual salary is $98217.

Paola declines all growth and advancement opportunities, is 'happy with where she is at' and only receives 2.4 per cent wage growth for the rest of her working life.

By making these decisions, at the age of 65 Paola will have earned $1298040 less than Daisy, and $385775 less than Masako over her working life. When it comes to retirement, her superannuation balance will be $77790 less than Masako and $215072 less than Daisy.

When we first glance at Paola's situation — not advancing in her job life and not increasing her salary beyond the standard nominal wage growth increase — we might wonder about her competency and question her drive, motivation, employee value and other factors.

But that would be a hasty and wrong assumption. Unfortunately, Paola's situation is not unusual and, in fact — from my experience — is quite the norm. On the other hand, it's Daisy's story that's rare. Paola's situation also represents many women working in lower paid and feminised industries. Consider retail, healthcare and women working for themselves.

• • •

Before we point the finger, take a good look around and see who might fall into Paola's or Masako's category. Your friends, neighbour, aunt, sister, children's best friend's mum? You would not know, but I know the reality is high. Paola's story is similar to the person from scenario 1: the one who received no salary increase for 10 years. I meet and interview people in these situations every week.

We shouldn't be quick to judge—instead, we should help. A lack of self-belief and confidence erodes our ability to ask for more—or even what is owed and fair. It also stops us from sharing our stories with friends and those who might be able to help. Instead, we pretend everything is okay, and that we are happy with our lot.

Make no mistake, low self-confidence and diminished self-esteem can be profoundly debilitating. The longer we stay in this predicament, the worse it becomes and the harder it is to find our way out. It's pervasive and, like quicksand, difficult to escape unless you act quickly.

Even with extensive coaching and practice, many individuals struggle to initiate conversations with their boss about critical matters such as salary and working conditions, let alone have the confidence to put their hat in the ring for a promotion.

It might seem that they prefer things to stay the way they are—familiar and safe—even if that means endlessly existing in the status-quo. How, then, do we expect someone like Paola—trapped in this psychological state—to contribute to meetings, be seen or heard, or put their hand up? It is a self-perpetuating cycle of self-doubt and inactivity.

Being unable to advocate for yourself stems from a deeper fear of rejection and inadequacy, reinforcing a pattern of invisibility and stagnation. Breaking free from this cycle requires not just external encouragement but a fundamental shift in self-perception and the courage to face your fears head-on.

I interview people who would rather resign from their job than ask for an increase in their salary or wages. They would prefer to ask a total stranger for more money rather than their boss, despite 'loving their boss and job'. For every person shaking their head in disbelief at what I am writing, there are 10 nodding away in silent affirmation.

At this juncture, instead of encouraging women to come out of their shells, take charge and employ every other self-empowerment action I can think of, I turn to corporations and organisations. You know who these women are. Show them some kindness, compassion, consideration and encouragement. Make your environment one where such conservations are easy. Resist the temptation to take advantage of the reduced salary levels, and have your actions reflect both heart and integrity. Remember, it could be someone close to you and for whom you care about deeply.

The three examples of Daisy, Masako and Paola portray simple but real-life situations. Daisy is applying herself and committed to building the best financial future she can. Masako has potential but hasn't really applied herself to the fullest. Paola, of course, also has potential (we all have potential) but is possibly suffering from significantly low self-esteem.

We all make life choices, and if we contently choose to be Paola or Masako let's do so from the right choice, not diminished self-power.

If you are in your mid 40s or 50s and reading this, don't despair. You have time. The principle for better decision making remains, and I hope the effect of compound earnings never goes away! Figures 5.1 to 5.3 might assure you of that.

Summing up Daisy's, Masako's and Paola's lifetime earnings, we see that:

- the total difference in lifetime earnings between Daisy and Masako is $912 265
- the total difference in lifetime earnings between Daisy and Paola is $1 298 040
- the total difference in lifetime earnings between Masako and Paola is $385 775.

The building of superannuation is critical. And with longer life expectancy, we all need it! Which brings us to the all-important topic of retirement.

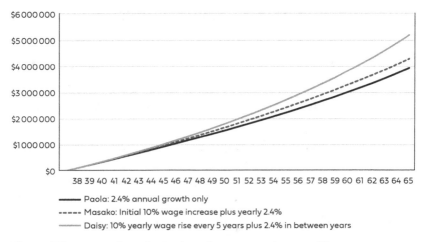

Figure 5.1: accumulated earnings by year up to age 65

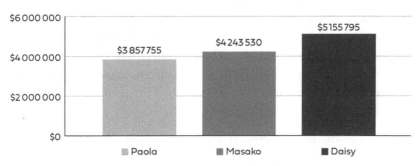

Figure 5.2: total accumulated salary earnings from 38 years to age 65

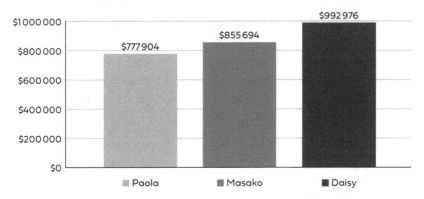

Figure 5.3: total accumulated superannuation from 38 years to age 65

A comparison of Daisy's, Masako's and Paola's accumulated superannuation shows that:

- the total difference in accumulated superannuation between Daisy and Masako is $137 282

- the total difference in accumulated superannuation between Daisy and Paola is $215 072

- the total difference in accumulated superannuation between Masako and Paola is $77 790.

Financial security in retirement

Currently, women retire with $136 000 less in superannuation than men. Many of us put thoughts of retirement on the back burner: *I'll deal with it later* or *When I get closer to retiring.* It's understandable, as no matter our age, retirement does feel far away. Maybe it is wishful thinking because, rightly or wrongly, retirement does come with its negative connotations, most of which are associated with the end-of-life journey and the unknown. The thing is, retirement comes whether we want it or not.

With the predisposition of being ageist, Western society's view on older generations doesn't help the cause. The ABS's magic barometer has '65' as being old. It gets considerably worse, with researchers commonly defining older workers as those over 50.[89] If we go back in time just a little to the *2005 Year Book Australia,* older workers were defined as those aged 45 to 64.[90] I wish we held the older generation in the same high regard as traditional Eastern Asian cultures: pedestal-like and revered. Maybe then we might openly embrace life's next stage and prepare for it.

Part of the issue in dealing with retirement is financial uncertainty. In fact, the main determinant of when to retire is financial security. That's why it's so sad to hear that 31 per cent of retired women rely on their partner's income to meet their living costs at retirement.[91] According to the Australian Human Rights

Commission, on average women retire with $157 050 in super and men with $270 710.[92] So, even in retirement we have diminished financial independence.

The Association of Superannuation Funds of Australia (AFSA) says to retire 'comfortably', a single person needs $595 000 and a couple $690 000.[93] These figures assume retirement at age 67 through to 92 (the word they use is 'expire'—admittedly, disconcerting to read), that you own your home with no mortgage and that you can access some of the Age Pension provided by the government.

Personally, I find these figures too conservative. Perhaps it's because I envision a more comfortable retirement, but I don't think that's the case—I'm simply being realistic. Moreover, why is there a difference in figures between a single person and a couple of only $95 000 over a 25-year period? I understand the concept of shared resources and economies of scale, but this doesn't seem to account for individual expenses such as clothing, food, entertainment and travelling—let alone medical costs. It's only an additional $3800 a year! Perhaps it's just the realist in me.

Breaking the figures down further, the story doesn't get much better. For individuals aged 60 to 64 in June 2023 the average superannuation balance for males was $338 700 and for females the average was $261 000. A significant shortfall for both parties, but especially so for females.

There's more. If you are 50 to 54 and a male, you have $289 900 in your superannuation fund and females have $191 400. And if you are 45 to 49, males have $237 200 and females $158 100.[94]

If you think the government Age Pension will be your saviour, consider the following: at the time of writing, the full Age Pension is around $29 028 a year for singles and $43 753 a year for couples.[95] Thoughts of supplementing your income through working part-time, casually or one or two days a week, might need reconsideration. Know that for every dollar you earn a fortnight over $204, the Age Pension is reduced by 50 cents, and each dollar of combined income over $360 per fortnight will reduce the pension by 50 cents.[96]

It doesn't give much flexibility, or many options. Should we have to, though? Surely, by that age, all of us should be able to live a comfortable, safe and secure retirement until we 'expire'.

It's not the case, though, especially if you are a woman. Currently, women over 55 years of age are the fastest growing group of homeless people in Australia. The research also shows that most of these women experiencing homelessness have never been homeless before.[97] The Australian Human Rights Commission defines homelessness as not just a lack of access to shelter. It goes on to say it includes the lack of safety, security and stability, as well as the inability to control your living space.[98]

The link between the lack of financial security and poor retirement options for women cannot be a surprise or underestimated. These are our mothers and grandmothers and if we don't start to consider our future and retirement, it might also be us. We can't continue to put our heads in the sand. Instead, we have to evaluate, plan and prepare.

It's not an insurmountable task. It can be achieved with micro decisions and some courage. We know women are in this position because we earn less than men, which is the whole point of this book! What you earn directly correlates to your superannuation.

By 1 July 2025, the employer superannuation contribution rate will be 12 per cent. In 2025, if you are 40 years of age and manage to negotiate an increase of $5000 that year, and retire at 67, you will have contributed an extra $29 000 to your superannuation, through extra contributions of $16 200 (at a conservative growth rate of 4 per cent). That one discussion with your boss or company has contributed more than 21 per cent towards closing the $136 000 superannuation gap.

Consider making salary sacrifice contributions to top up your super. This is also referred to as a reportable employer super contribution (RESC), which is 'an extra superannuation payment requested by an employee and made by an employer, over and above the normal super (SG) contribution'.[99] Even at 1 per cent, it can make a difference over time. For consistency, using numbers already supplied, with the average annual salary at $98 217, it means a deduction of $982 per year from your salary to go to the fund. That's $18.88 a week, pre-tax, so in real terms, after an average tax rate of 24 per cent, it is $14.35. That's roughly three regular-sized lattes a week, or one sandwich or a McDonald's Double Filet-O-Fish small meal deal at $13.20 with some very small change. We might be better off losing the latter anyway, so it's a win–win all round.

Note: you pay a 15 per cent concessional tax on the extra contribution. However, that 1 per cent contribution of $982 at age 40 will mean an additional $40 000 plus when you retire, using 67 as the assumed retirement age. I am applying the same conservative growth rate of 4 per cent and, for simplicity, assuming your salary remains the same. Of course, this won't be the case, so the extra superannuation contribution will grow as your salary does. Additionally, I am only using the 1 per cent contribution of $982, not considering previous or other contributions.

What of your employer? Many organisations offer employer additional super. The next time you want to change jobs, build employer additional superannuation contribution to your ideal new job requirements list. Get financially savvy with every aspect of your job and working life.

A major factor in women's superannuation discrepancy is attributed to time taken off for caring responsibilities, typically maternity leave, raising a family and even looking after elderly parents. For women on maternity leave, there is the Parental Leave Pay scheme, but it applies only for a limited time and previously didn't cover superannuation payments. The good news is that effective 1 July 2025, superannuation will be paid on the Parental Leave Pay scheme.

The Parental Leave Pay scheme is only available for a short period of time: what about the rest of the time taken away from the workforce? If you have a partner, discuss a spousal contribution. This is a voluntary after-tax contribution to your super fund. Your partner may be eligible to receive tax offsets.

Of course, it's hard enough being on one income and raising a family, let alone adding to the pressure of an after-tax contribution for something that is 'so far away' in the future. But it is still worth having the conversation. You never know what will happen later in life, and we all need security.

The other alternative is to look at contribution splitting. This is where your partner splits some of their super and transfers it to your superannuation fund. Typically, this is done via the employer's contribution and is arranged through the super fund. You need to check with the fund, as not all funds do it.

These conversations are important. It's not just for financial security but also independence. If you can't have the conversation at home about your worth, value and contribution, how will you have it with your employer when asking for the salary, advancement, promotion or opportunity you deserve?

The naysayers

So, you have read the chapter, considered the facts, triple-checked the data and researched again, just to be sure. Yet something still niggles at you … That's what it is: surely the formula can be applied to men as well, so they can make better, stronger decisions? It does, and to the men I say 'you're welcome'!

Although, I'm not so sure it will give men that much of a step up. Men have been using this concept forever. They were born with it. I've already unpacked plenty of research in the preceding chapters, but here's some more to consider. Despite abilities being the same, a study by Cornell University found that 'men overestimate their abilities and performance, while women underestimate both'.[100] Additionally, men negotiate about four times as often as women.[101]

Take charge of your million-dollar future

Despite possessing remarkable talents and capabilities, it is an often-overlooked truth that many women frequently miss opportunities to earn more. This is due to societal norms and biases, but is also attributed to internal barriers. These barriers, rooted in self-perception and internalised limitations, can be as formidable as any external obstacle.

Internal doubt stifles ambition and deters women from seizing opportunities that could elevate their professional and financial status. The journey to overcoming these internal barriers begins with self-awareness and a deliberate shift in mindset.

By recognising their inherent value and embracing their right to assert their worth, women can transform these internal limitations into strengths. The path to financial empowerment lies not only in breaking external barriers, but also in fostering an inner resilience and confidence.

Having the independence, for me, was a game changer.

NAGI MAEHASHI,
ON FINANCIAL INDEPENDENCE

Chapter 6

FALSE BELIEFS AND TRAPS

There is a world of opportunity. So many options to live and love life to the fullest. But false beliefs and actions can stop us from taking action.

In exploring life's opportunities, I couldn't help but be drawn to a novel from 1963, *The Bell Jar*, by American writer and poet Sylvia Plath. Its clever title application and symbolism are too poignant not to mention. A bell jar is a glass dome used in science laboratories to display an object and, at the same time, hold or enclose said object.

The Bell Jar is set in the 1950s. Like the wordsmithing of the title 'She's Price(d)less', Plath's title is also evocative. Throughout the novel, Plath highlights the societal expectations imposed on women and the often conflicting roles they were expected to fulfil.

In *The Bell Jar*, the lead protagonist, Esther Greenwood, has a vision of a fig tree. Each branch and fig represents the many different life paths: a mother, career woman, artist, traveller, athlete and many, many more possibilities. Every fig extends, opening to more choices and possibilities. The options are endless, beyond all limitations, with not a constraint in sight. Or, as Plath writes, 'from the tip of every branch, like a fat purple fig, a wonderful future beckoned and winked'.[102]

Yet, Esther is paralysed by the fear that choosing one fig (option), one path in life, means sacrificing all the others. With the burden from others of what she 'should' do and the pressure to succeed with whatever choice, Esther is panicked. Crippled by indecision, the figs can only beckon invitingly for so long before they wither away, each one dying with the promise of a life she could have had.

I saw my life branching out before me like the green fig tree in the story. From the tip of every branch, like a fat purple fig, a wonderful future beckoned and winked. One fig was a husband and a happy home and children, and another fig was a famous poet and another fig was a brilliant professor, and another fig was Ee Gee, the amazing editor, and another fig was Europe and Africa and South America, and another fig was Constantin and Socrates and Attila and a pack of other lovers with queer names and offbeat professions, and another fig was an Olympic lady crew champion, and beyond and above these figs were many more figs I couldn't quite make out. I saw myself sitting in the crotch of this fig tree, starving to death, just because I couldn't make up my mind which of the figs I would choose. I wanted each and every one of them, but choosing one meant losing all the rest, and, as I sat there, unable to decide, the figs began to wrinkle and go black, and, one by one, they plopped to the ground at my feet.[103]

The fig tree of today, illustrated in figure 6.1, also has boundless possibilities, even more than in Esther's time. And the modern-day Esther is still conflicted. Our indecisions, frozen by fear, worry or the quiet hope that someone else will choose for us, allows others to take the figs we leave behind. Our dreams of our life's path are confounded by societal expectations of what should be.

Sometimes, and perhaps often, these expectations are ones we place on ourselves. And, occasionally, we even use them (unconsciously) to justify why 'we can't'.

False beliefs and traps

Figure 6.1: life's boundless opportunities

These are our false beliefs and traps, also seen as our blind spots. Esther had them, and we all carry them. Except, the false beliefs we hold onto as just and real are quietly contributing to a lifetime of missed opportunities, including the million-dollar gap in earnings. If you want to close that gap, the key to the formula may be...you.

In this chapter, I gently peel back the 'protective' layers that hold us captive, those false beliefs, like Esther's, that stop us from making small, incremental yet brave and meaningful decisions to pursue 'what could be'. It is a chapter of awareness and honesty.

So, when reading chapter 6, be aware of the potential for cognitive dissonance. You might rationalise or downplay your experiences or circumstances to justify your decisions. It's a protective instinct we use. It's also one of the layers I try to pry apart!

Surprising facts: what you need to know about false beliefs

- False beliefs come from social networks, not facts.
- 'The earth is flat' is one of the most well-known false beliefs.
- False beliefs are views we hold true even when unsupported or contradicted with evidence.
- A limiting belief is a belief about yourself that restricts you in some way.
- The 'illusory truth effect' is when people are more likely to believe false information after repeated exposure, even if they initially knew it was untrue.

Let's begin with a seemingly straightforward yet telling story to better understand the unyielding nature of false beliefs. This story, while not about gender, underscores the resilience of false beliefs—how they persist even when confronted with clear evidence to the contrary.

'All Aussies have blue eyes'

After completing my Japanese studies, I went to Japan to further develop my language skills. I did numerous different jobs and one of them was as a golf caddy. I had never stepped foot on a golf course before, yet here I was guiding four Japanese guests at a time (always male) around a gorgeous course just outside of Nagoya. The club had a strict dress code of pale blue overalls, an orange hard hat and sparkling, whiter-than-white towels attached to our belts for cleaning clubs and golf balls. So important was the presentation that we even had to wear white gloves. But the one area we had free rein to choose, was our sunglasses. Taking advantage of the liberty, I wore round, gold-rimmed glasses with sky-blue lenses, which were, of course, fashionable at the time.

By that time, my Japanese language skills were strong enough to handle my job and daily interactions. One day, I greeted my guests in Japanese, and the lead guest pointed his driver at me and, smiling warmly and confidently declared to his colleagues, 'All Australians have blue eyes.' In polite Japanese, I responded, 'Actually, I have green eyes.'

He stared at me, unfazed, and repeated in English, 'All Australians have blue eyes.' I smiled, removed my sunglasses, and said, 'No, I really have green eyes. These are just sunglasses.' The guest was disbelieving and continued to assert 'all Australians have blue eyes' as he led his friends and green-eyed caddy down the fairway.

The golfer's comment wasn't meant to be harmful in any way. The story about this brief encounter, placed in a different culture and happening so long ago, may sound truly trivial, but it portrays perfectly the power of false beliefs. No matter how convincing the evidence and facts we present are, people still seem to stick with their perceptions.

If you think this story belongs to a bygone era, you might be surprised. It is not an isolated case. It could be any other person from any corner of the world. It could be an Australian golfer.

We see and experience many instances when individuals in our society struggle to see beyond gender-based stereotypes. These false beliefs, whether about eye colour, competence or leadership ability, are not just innocent misconceptions. The challenge, then, is not just to present evidence but to also change the underlying perceptions.

False beliefs often stick around not because they are true or sound smart but because they seem easy.

Additionally, it is not hard to believe a good story and it is easier than to dig deeper for validity. But, here is the truth: if we don't stop to question these beliefs, we lose the chance to understand what's really happening. It's not just an intellectual exercise; it's about living a life knowing what is shaping our decisions and our views.

> *As you read chapter 6, will you remain stubborn to your beliefs or allow some dislodging of what might not be accurate and true? Some of the false beliefs won't be so obvious. That's their purpose.*
>
> *Prepare for some internal questioning, re-questioning and reflection. Even if it's uncomfortable, that's good; it can also be a sign of growth.*

What's wrong with false beliefs?

Let's explore some false beliefs and traps, test them and hold them accountable. These are the outdated, unwelcome beliefs we drag around with us—heavy and disabling, cumbersome, and supermarket trolley-like—the ones with the bung wheel that keeps trying to track you in the direction you don't want to go.

False beliefs aren't harmless, they carry consequences. If we want a better, more equal world, we must start questioning some of the tenets we have always taken for granted.

Let's start with the false belief I hear most from people...

'It's okay for you...'

I've often thought this when receiving advice. It might have been a parent, a teacher, a lecturer or an old boss as they sat there sharing their thoughts and trying to guide me. I read a similar look in the eyes of my team at times as I am desperately trying to motivate and encourage them to stretch themselves or be brave. Their eyes say it all: *It's okay for you.*

It's the same when I coach and mentor people. I know they have the skills and abilities. I know what they need to say, how to say it and how best to present themselves. Yet, their mindset and look are identical, silently conveying the same message: *It's okay for you.*

'It's okay for you' is code for:

- 'You don't know what it is like.'
- 'Your life is different or blessed.'
- 'You've got it easy.'
- 'You are more talented/skilled/capable/smarter than me.'
- 'You cannot possibly know how hard it is for me.'
- 'You don't know what I am going through, struggling with or feeling.'
- 'You make it sound so simple, but you don't see the complexity of my situation.'
- 'Your advice might work for others, but not me.'
- 'It's easy for you to preach change when your life seems so put together.'
- 'You've probably never had to fight this hard—no wonder you think change is simple.'
- 'You can afford to be optimistic because you've never faced the kind of setbacks I have.'
- 'What you are asking of me is too difficult.'

- 'No matter how hard I try, it never works.'

- 'I don't want to go there again. It's better I don't put myself in that place.'

I bet some of you are nodding and, as you are reading, are even thinking, *Yeah, it's okay for you; you have written a book on the subject.*

But I do know what it's like. I know what it's like to be swallowed by self-doubt, to believe you are not smart enough, or good enough. I know what it feels like to think, 'I'm slow to pick things up', 'I'm not cut out to do this', 'Maybe I should quit because I feel like I am failing' and 'I can't ask that question and look stupid'. The self-limiting beliefs and negative rhetoric are endless. They chip away at your self-esteem, slowly dismantling your confidence. It's a disease unto itself.

I spent 5 years studying part-time for my MBA. For the first three of those, I never asked a single question in class. Most of the students were male: accountants, bankers, lawyers and engineers. They put their hand up, asked many questions and contributed. They did nothing wrong; they were just confident and self-assured. Kudos to them. It was my issue. I was intimated and had carried enormous self-doubt.

Truthfully, I even wondered how I was allowed into the MBA program in the first place, convinced they would relook at my application and, in horror, discover the marks from my undergraduate degree. I had visions of the lovely course instructor (Geoff) taking me aside, embarrassed and hushedly explaining that there had been a mistake and they had no idea how I was allowed in.

By the time I reached the final year, only the top 30 per cent had qualified to be there. I deserved to be in that final master's year. I'd worked hard, really hard. Guess what though, even after all that hard work, effort, tears and sacrifice, when I graduated, I still felt 'lucky'. I was relieved and thankful, but I never really felt I earned my place. That's what years of damaging, self-limiting beliefs does to you.

I recognise now that it wasn't my abilities that held me back, but the power of self-doubt. Most concerning was recognising that no amount of hard-earned success can erase the shadows of insecurities. I have since learned you must work at these — and consistently.

So, yes, it is okay for me because I do know what it's like. Not just from this small example, but many experiences. I also know what it's like to work through the pain parts, the horrible discomfort and the raw exposure of your fears and perceived inadequacies. However, from repeatedly putting myself in these situations, I also know the benefits:

- personal growth and emotional strength
- overall strength, power and faith in abilities
- a deeper understanding of yourself
- reduced stress and increased capacity to do more
- ability to help others.

The next time you think *It's okay for you*, reconsider. You don't know that person's circumstances, experiences and the struggles they have faced to reach the point where they can share their knowledge and advice with you. It's an unfair assumption to think *It's okay for you*, because assuming that their path has been easy is not only unfair but also dismissive of their journey. It's more than likely that they know exactly what it's like.

Saying or thinking *It's okay for you*, and the like, does you no favours. It's the kind of thinking that shuts down curiosity and openness. Instead of thinking *What can I learn from this person?*, you're thinking *There's nothing I can learn*. It should be one of those mind messages you train yourself to erase.

Instead of assuming, ask yourself: What might I learn from their experiences?

'Why are others successful and I'm not?'

None of us is immune to this kind of thinking. It's reductive though.

This kind of thinking assumes the other person has done nothing to deserve their 'success'. You don't know how hard they worked, what sacrifices were made or even how successful they really are. It could be just the surface you see. It is why I am cautious and even nervous about the pervasiveness of social media.

Social media often presents a highly curated and unrealistic version of a person's life, showcasing only their best moments and hiding their struggles. It is the same for celebrities you revere, friends and those 'distant friends' you hardly know. We know this, right? Yet we can't help but continue to compare.

Comparing ourselves is normal, and we have always done it. Yet, it's unrealistic to compare ourselves out of context and to the degree we do now, unfiltered—excuse the pun. Focusing on others' perceived successes can distract us from our own personal growth and unique journey, potentially causing us to overlook our own achievements.

In 1954, psychologist Leon Festinger proposed the theory of 'social comparison', whereby people look to determine their self-worth by comparing themselves to others.[104] It is the tendency to use other people as sources of information to determine how we are doing ourselves. There are three types of social comparison: upward social comparison, downward social comparison and lateral social comparison.

Festinger discovered that, in general, more people socially compare themselves upward; that is, to people of higher social status. You can see this phenomenon playing out in contemporary life on social media. Because posts on social media only display the best parts of people's lives, they represent unrealistic expectations. This is why social comparison is so much stronger on social media and also leads to unhealthy consequences.[105]

The MIT Sloan School of Management presents some truly concerning research. Concurrent with Facebook's meteoric expansion there has been growing concern over the mental wellbeing of adolescents and young adults. 'The researchers posit that social comparison with peers is behind those results, and it is an effect that appears to grow stronger as people are exposed to Facebook for greater lengths. The effects seem to increase with time.'[106]

It can be similar when you compare yourself at work to someone who seems to have it all. For example, the woman working and juggling home commitments. She has a career and a well-paid job, seems to have it altogether, never falters in meetings or presentations, and makes it out on time for important family and children's events.

> *Don't compare. Instead, ask her how she does it.*

You might feel tired, worn out, stressed and like a walking wreck trying to manage it all. Maybe she does too. The child's Weet-Bix vomit on your lapel, she has it too. She learned to wear patterned shirts a long time ago, and no, it's not silk, that's way too much effort to launder. It's viscose that can be thrown in the machine, and the best part is, it doesn't need ironing. Or maybe she has found great support at home, or some new technology saving her time at home and at work. All of us find our own life hacks and ways of coping. It's okay if you haven't figured it out yet and, honestly, I am not sure any of us truly master it. If it looks that way, it's an illusion. And maybe, it's about learning those small wins that makes the chaos a little more manageable

'What about the other false beliefs and traps we fall into?'

Yes, there are plenty more. Here are a few.

1. *The belief that we must choose one over the other*

It is understandable that many women feel they have to choose between having a career or having a family. As for Esther, it's the paralysing fear that choosing one means losing out on the other. How did we come to that conclusion?

Men certainly don't. Why can't we be a mother and have a career? Is it the expectation that home, caring and domestic responsibilities sit primarily with women? Don't believe me? We already do 2.6 times more domestic work than men.[107]

Look at Leila McKinnon, Kristina Karlsson, Julia Ross and Professor Fiona Wood, all women who work and have a family. As Fiona said, perhaps 'I overcompensated with six children'. Their advice on this topic is:

- You need help at home: fathers, friends, grandparents.

- You need help at work: understanding bosses and colleagues and a supportive environment.

- Speak up. Don't assume an unfair amount of responsibility.

- Outsource if you can afford it. Anything: nannies, cleaners, washing, babysitters.

- Prioritise: work out what is important at that time and work from there.

- There is a time for everything. It's just not all at once.

2. *The belief that you can't be successful and liked*

It is one of the most damaging beliefs women hold. This false dilemma, rooted in social pressures, suggests that being assertive, ambitious and a leader are traits that are inherently in conflict with femininity and likability.

Women are often led to believe that pursuing career goals too aggressively will make them unfeminine and/or unlikable. However, the qualities that make a good leader, such as confidence, decisiveness and resilience, are not inherently male or female; they are human qualities. The myth that these traits are incompatible with being liked or respected as a woman is a barrier that must be dismantled.

If you don't believe me, take it from a male CEO's perspective. Phil Kearns' comments on women in business and leadership roles are: 'Be who you are and be authentic'. He also says, one of the great strengths of his business is having women on his team. 'They bring a different approach, view and an alternative perspective to problems. They think about things differently and have a heightened sense of empathy. '

3. *The belief that success will come as long as you work hard and keep your head down*

I'm here to tell you success won't come just from working hard, being conscientious and assuming you will be seen. Success on these terms is never a given and it will never be handed to you. Maybe in a perfect world, but that is not our world. While hard work is important, the belief that it is the only factor in achieving success ignores the reality of systemic biases and the necessity of strategic self-advocacy. We are often socialised to believe that self-promotion is boastful or that asking for what you deserve is somehow ungrateful. In reality, understanding one's worth and advocating for it is not just a right, it's essential for breaking through the glass ceilings that still exist.

4. *The belief in the perfect work–life balance*

Many women are led to believe that career success must be perfectly balanced with family life and that anything less is a sign of failure. This belief is not only unrealistic but also damaging. It sets an impossible standard that can lead to feelings of guilt and inadequacy.

Realistically, is there balance anywhere? So why do we carry the pressure for the precarious, unattainable balance between home, family, work and everything else? It's absurd. There is no single formula for balancing work and life; it is a dynamic process that changes with circumstances, and perfection is neither attainable nor necessary. What's important is finding a rhythm that works and understanding that some sacrifices are inevitable and do not diminish one's success or worth.

The pursuit of a perfect balance often becomes a barrier, causing women to doubt their choices or hold back from opportunities that might tip the scales temporarily but leads to long-term fulfilment.

Additionally, enlist help at home. Negotiate shared responsibilities. It is a long-outdated belief to expect domestic and caring responsibilities that sit within the metrics of 'home balance' to be a woman's job.

You are not Superwoman. Superwoman identity refers to a woman who performs a combination of multiple concurrent full-time roles such as wife, mother, worker, homemaker and caregiver.[108] They are 'double-burdened' with the responsibility of fulfilling both their domestic and career obligations—and guess what? Because they are superwomen, they do it all and they do it well.[109]

> *Here's the truth: while the idea of Superwoman might inspire, she is an archetype. She isn't meant to represent a standard we must meet, and neither should the unrealistic expectations that come with this myth. We can celebrate strength and capability without burdening ourselves with impossible standards.*

5. *The belief that success should be achieved without help*

Another pervasive 'myth' is that true success is something that must be earned entirely through one's own efforts, and that seeking help or mentorship is a sign of weakness or an admission of inadequacy. This idea is deeply ingrained in the notion of individualism and the 'self-made' narrative, and it is particularly harmful to women, who face unique challenges and barriers in the workplace and life.

No-one achieves success alone. Seeking out mentors, building a supportive network and asking for help when needed are not only wise but also necessary strategies for overcoming obstacles and advancing in the workplace. Men do this exceptionally well.

The idea that asking for help undermines one's success is an incorrect belief that perpetuates isolation and limits the potential for growth and advancement. Women should be encouraged to leverage every resource available to them, understanding that collaboration and support are key components of success.

These beliefs serve as invisible shackles holding women back from financial and career success.

Avoiding the traps

What about some of the traps we fall into when we listen too much to what others think? I advocate seeking advice and help from 'others'. However, it can be a fine line between what seems like 'tough' yet valuable insight and advice and that of negative rhetoric. Don't let the fears of others or their biases hold you back from reaching your dreams or potential

Professor Fiona Wood: 'I was told women don't do surgery'

What if Fiona Wood had listened to societal expectations?

It's been over 20 years since the Bali bombings, and yet, despite the length of time, I am sure, the memory of that event will never leave the minds of any Australian alive at that time. In October 2002, Fiona led the medical team when the biggest contingent of survivors from the 2002 Bali bombings arrived at Royal Perth Hospital. Fiona oversaw the treatment of more people in the aftermath of the Bali bombings than any other person in Australia. Of the 28 people who arrived on that tarmac from Bali, she was able to save 25.

Fiona's greatest contribution and enduring legacy is her work with co-inventor Marie Stoner, pioneering an innovative 'spray-on skin' technique. Today, the technique

(continued)

> is used worldwide. Fiona was named a Member of the Order of Australia (AM) in 2003. In 2004 she was awarded the Western Australia Citizen of the Year award for her contribution to medicine in the field of burns research. She was then named Australian of the Year for 2005. She is an Australian National Living Treasure.
>
> Fiona shared with me, 'There are plenty of people who say you can't do things. But you don't have to listen to them. It's their frame of reference and judgement. Not yours. Yes, I was told women don't do surgery, but I choose not to listen.'
>
> Thank goodness she didn't listen.

Leila McKinnon also 'didn't listen'. She didn't listen to those around her telling her how hard it was going to be. Leila didn't give in when the challenges seemed insurmountable. I'm glad she felt all those self-doubts, worries of failure and tears at times, and then said, 'No, I'm going to do it anyway.'

> ## Leila McKinnon: why wouldn't you want to be a journalist?
>
> Leila McKinnon is a 30-year veteran in media, a tough, cutthroat industry and one that has traditionally been heavily male dominated, especially at the decision-making helm. Leila has navigated a successful career in Australian journalism and is one of the most likeable, competent and warm journalists on TV today.
>
> Leila has interviewed some of the highest profile people in the world, from royalty to seven prime ministers. Did I

mention Beyoncé? She interviewed her twice! But that's not where this is going.

I get the sense from Leila that she got into journalism for the adventure and storytelling. For someone who mentioned at the beginning of her career not being great 'with confrontation', I think she has that down pat. Leila told me how, in the earlier days, she would take on assignments such as chasing con men into country towns and nearly being run out of town by their friends. Coming close to being punched, and genuinely terrified. But she would then go back for more stories.

Her producer would send her in for one story, 'but get three while you are there if you can'.

'I always did,' she said.

Leila was one of the journalists covering the Solomon Islands coup and speaks about staying in a beaten-up old shed with holes in the wall and being too scared to sleep while the coup was raging outside. Then having the militia race at her, the cameraman and the producer with guns.

In the same breath as she finished the sentence, she then said how grateful she was for the producer she worked with. 'She was tough but so supportive and great to me. I was hopeless at looking after myself. There was a time I had to go away for a story, and she got my car serviced and cleaned for me. I've had some great supportive women around me.'

Leila didn't tell me this, but I read somewhere when I was doing my research that one of her favourite interviews was meeting members of the 100-year-old club. She spoke with them about the Depression and World War I years and was so grateful to meet them.

Self-doubt

We all have it. No-one is immune from self-doubt. As for the highly accomplished and successful people I interviewed, yes, they too had and continue to carry self-doubt and, yes, even Phil Kearns. Here is a little secret...when I asked the question, 'Do you ever have self-doubt?', it was an emphatic 'yes'. There was no hesitation, side-stepping dalliance or avoidance. It was answered in a way of, 'Of course, we all do.'

What I have learned, however, is it is what you do with that little whisper of doubt that pops into your head. How much airtime do you allow it? Here are some of the interviewees' thoughts on the topic of self-doubt.

Fiona Wood said to me straight out, 'I still have it now.' She then went on to say that in the greater context of being a health professional it is important to understand the 'profound impact and influence on others'. She said to me, 'so you shouldn't take that lightly'. Later in the conversation she added that she knows things like 'imposter syndrome can be crippling, but a healthy dose of humility is not bad'.

Kristina Karlsson said to me, 'Self-doubt is the number one killer of every dream.' She talked to me about goals and dreams and the impact self-doubt can have. She said, 'People are often worried about what other people think and they carry that with them. Or they focus on how hard it will be or that they can't or "I'm not there yet". The problem is you are basing your thoughts on where you are today. You are not thinking of where I can be and how I can.'

Phil Kearns' answer was, 'I mean all the time. That's why resilience is so important.'

What happens when it all gets too much?

It happens—and to all of us. It would be ignorant of me to say, 'Keep going' and 'Don't give up', when the reality is that it's not always about pushing through—sometimes it's about knowing when to change course and make better decisions.

Kristina Karlsson is the consummate optimist and, yes, as the quintessential entrepreneur, she doesn't stay down for long. I was particularly intrigued to hear her take on whether sometimes it's the better decision to not keep going. Here is what she shared with me.

Kristina Karlsson: 'Yes, I've had a big failure'

I have to say, all through our chat Kristina never loses her enthusiasm, verve and beat.

I asked Kristina, 'Surely there are times when you have no choice, or it's best to "give up"?'

This is what she said, 'Sometimes, yes, absolutely, it's not always better to keep going. Sometimes there is also no choice. I've experienced this and had the hardest of times. The most challenging time was when I lost my business.'

Kristina walks me through this, saying that while she lost her business, she chose not to give up on everything else. She said to me, 'I thought, "I am not going down with the business. My life is so valuable, so I am going to make the most of it. I am going to work through it."'

Kristina admits, though, it took her a couple of years to work through everything — and with a lot of self-love.

Kristina's advice for other people, when faced with adversity or challenging times, is 'yes, it can be hard. If at the same time, you are dealing with young children, a child with special needs or going through something challenging yourself — ageing parents, losing someone, divorce, whatever that might be — then yes, it can be even tougher. You need a strong support network, family, partner, whatever that is, and take time for self-care and love'.

Sometimes it does all get too much and the better decision is to change direction. You can see from Kristina's story her outlook in the face of failure and the toughest of challenging times remained strong. She wouldn't let it define her or let it be her identity.

Kristina's story is a reminder that the path to success is almost never linear. It requires resilience, perseverance, a positive mindset and strong self-belief. This understanding can allow us to believe in our power, even in the face of failure, as we rewrite our own stories. In typical Kristina spirit, with just an element of mischief, she couldn't help but add, 'Mostly though, you just cannot give up!'

Closing the gender pay gap is not just about the money: it's about empowerment, autonomy and the ability for women to live life on their terms. Everyone should have the opportunity to fulfil their dreams.

Women can make a difference for themselves, and we should. We can't expect others to take up the baton if we are not doing so ourselves. That's one societal expectation I implore you to embrace. Otherwise, it's just wishful thinking.

Life is too short not to live our dream lives.

KRISTINA KARLSSON

Chapter 7

WHAT HE SAID: INSIGHTS AND ADVICE FOR MEN

One of the first things Phil Kearns said to me when I interviewed him was, 'I know the business world is dominated by men, so use us!'

> **In the nicest possible way, we are there to be used.**
> **Phil Kearns**

He went on, 'I would struggle to think of any man I know in business who would say, "I am not helping a woman." Those days are gone. In my world anyway and among the guys I deal with in business.'

Phil is true to his word. Before writing this book, I didn't know Phil. In considering who to approach for this book, I imagined Phil's multifaceted perspective as a successful CEO, a prominent public figure, ex-athlete, advocate for women's sports, and in his personal roles as a husband and father would offer invaluable insights. I asked a friend who knows Phil for an introduction. We spoke on the phone and within 5 minutes, Phil said, 'Sure, I'll do it, I'll help.'

Thank you, Phil!

I have been fortunate to have wonderful males in my life. My brilliant dad, beautiful brother, divinely aware and clever partner, and all my gorgeous, smart and funny male friends. They come with their faults, there is no doubt. As do I, in abundance. Have I experienced forms of gender bias from the important male figures and role models in my life? The answer is yes. All women have. It's ingrained in every facet of society.

My dad was born in Scotland in 1940, part of the silent generation with traditionalist values. If you have ever heard the term 'children should be seen and not heard', you will be familiar with the parenting of this generation. You had your place. And it was similar for women. Except my dad married my mum, an Australian-educated woman who wanted to work—and she did. I am sure there were many strained conversations on this topic and others.

For my parents' generation, my mother pursuing a career outside the home was not the norm and definitely viewed as advancement. In fact, from what I experienced in my upbringing, my parents were very progressive and we should give credit where and when it's due.

We make advancements as individuals, groups and the collective by being open, aware, compassionate and caring about those important to us. It shouldn't be hard to let go of established norms, practices and even beliefs when we see the hurt they might cause.

This chapter is addressed to men. It provides practical advice and shows how simple actions can affect change to help close the gender pay gap (a gentle reminder: it's a million dollars!). However, it doesn't do it without acknowledgement and respect for the role they have already and continue to play. In the continued fight for change, it's easy to overlook the distance we've already covered.

For the wonderful men out there, read on. Here's what you can do to assist your partner, daughter, mother, friends, colleagues and society. The first step is to be more aware, curious and informed.

Surprising facts: insights and advice for men

- Eighty-five per cent of women have experienced some form of sexual harassment.[110]

- Companies that have in place systems, practices and protocols committed to gender equity are more likely than ever to financially outperform companies that don't.

- 'Girls grow up with broader career goals in households where domestic duties are shared more equitably by parents.'[111]

- When fathers claim to endorse gender equality but don't perform household chores, their daughters are more likely to envision themselves in stereotypical 'female' occupations.[112]

- Companies in the top quartile for gender diversity on their executive teams were 21 per cent more likely to have above-average profitability than companies in the fourth quartile.[113]

Men, you own the joint

Some time ago, a friend convinced me to watch an interview with author and actress Fran Lebowitz. Her hilarious, grim, cynical social commentary was, of all things, obvious, especially in the gender stakes. Watching that interview, I let Fran's observations sink in. For me, her standout comment was:

'Men. They own the joint.'

And they still do.

Sometimes, all you need for clarity is one short, sharply worded sentence. It stuck with me. Men own, women rent. The analogy to and symbolism of the million-dollar gap can't be ignored.

Women need a stronger mark in the gender equity stake, and to do so, we need men right by our side, not ahead, not behind, but alongside, accompanying us the whole way. Closing the pay gap is not a female-only issue. We cannot bring about change on our own. It requires a collective effort.

Additionally, we don't need 'saving'. This would be reverting back to the unconscious bias and stereotyping of the hero and heroine. Or worse, Cinderella. We don't need a prince to come to our rescue. If using fable analogies, we seek a Fairy Godmother: someone who quietly enables and empowers, who believes in our potential and helps us realise it without the fanfare of saving the day.

Fathers: raising confident daughters and empathic sons

The role of a father carries profound significance. A father can shape his daughter's future by modelling respect and equality in his relationships, assuring her that the world holds no bounds for her dreams and nurturing a future where her aspirations know no limits. And when a father teaches his son the quiet strength of valuing women as equals, he plants roots of empathy and fairness within his son's heart.

It is in these gentle acts of guidance that a father shapes not just the lives of his children, but the fabric of the next generation, a generation that will carry forward the spirit of equity and respect. Fiona Wood, Julia Ross and Peta Credlin spoke emphatically about the importance of their upbringing to their roles now, their achievements and successes. These highly accomplished and successful women were imbued with the belief in their hearts and minds that the world was theirs.

It takes more than words though. As with all good role models, it's in the actions that intentions are validated. Studies show that when parents share domestic responsibilities they influence their children to have more equitable gender attitudes, particularly daughters. While a mother's gender and work equality beliefs are key factors in predicting a child's attitude towards gender, the strongest predictor of daughters' own professional ambitions is the fathers' approach to household chores.[114]

Research from the University of British Columbia shows 'fathers who help with household chores are more likely to raise daughters who aspire to less traditional, and potentially higher paying, careers'. Meanwhile, boys who observe this behaviour grow up to be men who support gender equality in their own relationships.[115]

Alyssa Croft, the lead author of the UBC study, observes, 'girls grow up with broader career goals in households where domestic duties are shared more equitably by parents'.[116] Croft also notes that when 'fathers endorsed gender equality but didn't perform household chores, their daughters were more likely to envision themselves in stereotypical female jobs'.[117]

The influence of fathers in raising confident daughters and empathetic sons cannot be overstated. Through daily actions and attitudes, fathers have the power to shape a future where gender equality is the norm, not the exception. The ripple effect extends beyond the family unit. As research consistently shows, the seemingly small choices fathers make in their everyday lives have profound impacts on their children's future aspirations, relationships and worldviews, ultimately helping to forge a more equitable and compassionate world for generations to come.

Peta Credlin on a father's influence

Peta Credlin shares a touching story from when she was four. She recalled how she could read well before going to school and that she was a confident child. It was her first day at her country school and there were only six students in her class. The teacher asked the question if anyone knew how to read or knew their ABCs. Peta put her hand up saying, 'I can read, I can read, and I know all my ABCs.' The teacher said 'no you can't'. Peta responded, 'well I can' and went up to the teacher's desk where *The Sun* newspaper (later to become the *Herald Sun*) was and started reading the first few lines. But instead of praise, the teacher tugged at her pinafore to sit down and told her, 'no-one likes a show off'.

Peta told me she cried when this happened (imagine a little four-year old girl on her first day at school!). Her dad picked her up after school that day and asked how her first day was. When Peta recounted the story, her dad told her she was to 'keep doing what she is doing'. For the following weeks, her dad made an effort to pick her up from school encouraging her each day. He would say, 'what happened today, did you say anything today? C'mon, you're going to say something tomorrow.' She told me, 'Dad turned it around from me feeling ashamed, to it being "our thing". And it's important that you understand here that my father left school after grade six, he had no secondary education, and it was something he felt keenly all his life. I don't think I properly understood that myself until I was much older, and even today it makes me very sad because he loved learning. Though he never really had that opportunity, he still managed to instill that love in me.'

> *'Dads are really powerful.'*
> **Peta Credlin**

The story of fathers and daughters is written in countless small moments, whether it's the shared laughter over breakfast or the quiet conversations like Peta's. This precious relationship reminds us that some of life's most profound impacts occur not in grand gestures, but in the steady presence of everyday love, and the unwavering belief in a daughter's potential.

Challenge all stereotypes: men supporting men

Men can redefine masculinity by embracing positive traits that promote gender equality and rejecting harmful stereotypes. We have spoken extensively about the harmful and often dangerous gender stereotyping applied to women. It sits unjustly with men as well. Men often grapple with societal expectations that can constrain their choices, behaviours and self-expression, frequently facing pressures to conform to narrow definitions of masculinity.

The divinely aware and clever partner I refer to at the beginning of the chapter is also sharp in wit. As he vacuumed the other day, he called out, mid-elongated sweep, smirk visible, 'Apparently, it's sexy — all the podcasts tell me this.' What do I say? The truth? It's not. Not when I do it and not when you do it.

Obviously, I am not going to lie. I also know his sarcasm and sardonic tone knows no bounds. It has probably reached Fran in New York and they are developing some off-Broadway skit about the ridiculousness of the statement, with discerning observations and perspicacious commentary. No, vacuuming is not sexy. But, it has to be done. Data from the OECD found that countries where men participate more equally in unpaid domestic work have higher rates of female workforce participation and smaller gender pay gaps.[118]

It's not all about the domestic and home responsibilities, although that is where the main gender stereotyping in relationships typically sits—and on both sides. Here are some other examples to explore. They might not pertain to you ... but maybe ...

- refusing to ask for directions or help when lost (my all-time personal favourite)
- expecting women to be solely responsible for meal planning and preparation
- dismissing hobbies or interests perceived as 'feminine'. For example, would you knit or play men's netball? Men's netball competitions have been in place since 1985
- refusing to wear certain colours or styles deemed 'unmanly'.

Or what about these:
- deriding other men for not conforming to certain masculine stereotypes
- suppressing emotions and vulnerability
- shying away from expressing affection
- insisting on being the one to drive, even when it's your partner's car
- not admitting you are sick due to a misguided sense of toughness.

Men can help dismantle harmful stereotypes by redefining what it means to be a man in modern society. A 'real man' in today's world is a good human. Men can support other men by not being derogatory when they step out of gender-confining roles.

Be a man about it

In comparison to 'stay-at-home mums', there are very few 'stay-at-home dads', or dads working part-time to balance the role of primary caregiver. In Australia, 'the number of stay-at-home fathers remains small, at about 4 to 5 per cent of two-parent families'.[119]

What would you say if your mate, brother, son or colleague decided to be a stay-at-home dad? Would you be supportive? Or perhaps poke some gender-based fun? Your jokes and words stick. If you think it doesn't matter or that 'blokes don't care about those things', it's not true and your mate is never going to admit to it. Because, like women, men are also conditioned. Conditioned to 'be a man about it'.

Don't assume your mate or colleague isn't interested in his career just because he decides to take extended parental leave, stay home and look after the family responsibilities or change countries to support his wife's career and her dream to work abroad. Don't be quick to judge a man as being less serious about his job if he chooses to leave work right on the dot of 5.00 pm to be home in time for dinner with the family. Or dedicates time to do the pickup or go to parent–teacher night.

We need to recognise and address the jokes that are not jokes, the derision and inferred gender biases, labelling, stereotyping and name-calling of men. Just as we do for women. Micro-aggressions like these have a negative impact on wellbeing, extending to mental health issues, lowered self-esteem and reduced confidence.

Evidence points to the negative impact of hegemonic masculinity on men's health.[120] Additionally, research studies show young Australian men disagree with outdated stereotypes of masculinity but feel pressure to conform in public. Men who are most constrained by harmful stereotypes of what it means to be a man report mental health issues and risky behaviour.[121]

Consider these examples of non-jokes and labelling that perpetuate harmful stereotypes for men:

- saying they are 'whipped' (a personal loathe)
- saying they are domesticated

- referring to the nappy bag as their 'manbag'
- saying they are on a short leash or henpecked
- saying they are soft when prioritising family, balance or anything outside of work or career
- referring to being on 'daddy-track' instead of career track.

Men have traditionally excelled at social bonding, and these connections remain vital for men's personal and professional relationships. As society evolves and our understanding of gender roles shifts, mutual support among men becomes essential for maintaining good mental health and wellbeing. Nurturing these relationships and offering each other encouragement paves the way for a more inclusive and progressive future.

Parental leave for fathers

Currently, in Australia, effective 1 July 2023, families have 100 parental-leave days to be shared, with a maximum of 90 days taken by each parent.[122] Research shows that fathers who take care of children in their early years are more likely to stay involved as their children grow up and men who engage with their children report better life satisfaction and physical and mental health.[123]

Scandinavian countries have long been the world leader in this area. Iceland stands as a stellar example, with its equal parental leave policy. This policy not only supports women in returning to work but also normalises men's involvement in childcare, breaking down long-standing gendered expectations. Studies from Nordic countries where shared parental leave is more common show a correlation between men taking parental leave and women's increased participation in the workforce, as well as a reduction in the gender pay gap.

In Sweden, parents are entitled to 480 days of paid parental leave, with each parent entitled to 240 of those days. Parents can transfer days to each other, but dads must take at least 90 days.[124] This part I love! Additionally, parental leave can be taken any time up until the child turns 12. Nordic research shows that men who take longer parental leave also take more responsibility at home.[125]

Having been brought up in Sweden, Kristina Karlsson stands as a prime example. Kristina spoke with me about coming out from Sweden to Australia in the late 1990s and said it was her first exposure to gender inequity. 'It was the first time I heard about it ... I never saw myself as different [from] a male and I was never treated differently because I was a girl or a woman. Because of that and my upbringing, I also never treated anyone else differently because they were a girl or boy.'

Parental leave for fathers is good for men and for their children. It also paves the way for transformative benefits for the gender pay gap. From a structural and societal perspective, if men can equally take parental leave, with no stigma or derision, and there is financial provision for it, there will be less discrimination about hiring women. C'mon, we know it exists.

The silent debate about hiring women at childbearing age and knowing *that* question is never allowed to be asked. I know it exists because companies continue to tell me. They hesitate, calling it 'strategic risk assessment'. Beneath the 'unspoken' lies the fear of unpredictability. What it means to accommodate both ambition and biology.

The tacit assumption that a woman's potential must be weighed against the unpredictability of her future, as if the act of bringing life into the world is somehow an obstacle rather than an extension of human progress. What does this say about our humanity when we have to have these conversations in whispers?

Be our ally ... and more

We need men as our allies. Friendship is one thing, being an ally is another. When it comes to gender equality, it is who stands by us, with us and is prepared to stand up and stand out. As a man, being noticed for your gender activism and support is the next level, where it provides tangible effects of change—and not just at work. A study from Boston Consulting Group (BCG) found that companies with male allies were more likely to have effective gender diversity programs, showing how men's involvement is not just about support but essential for systemic change.[126]

Allyship for the gender equality battle is not only a moral prerogative. It advances everyone's interests. A large and growing body of research shows that organisations with greater numbers of women, especially in leadership roles, perform better. A 2016 Peterson Institute for International Economics study of 22000 global companies found that as companies increased the number of women among board members and senior leaders, their profit margins increased as well.[127]

Many men have the positions of power and influence to advocate for equality and opportunity for women. By actively challenging stereotypes and biases in everyday conversations and micro-inequities, you support equality not just as a workplace value but a guiding principle in all aspects of life.

One of the most potent ways you can use your influence is through peer networks and influence. Holding other men accountable is a brave act. Just like you might have stuck up for your mates in the playground as a child, we need that from you now, in the employment arena.

'Worldwide research by BCG shows that among companies where men are actively involved in gender diversity, 96 per cent report progress compared to only 30 per cent where men are not involved.'[128] Through genuine respect and fairness in their relationships, men can nurture a culture where equality and opportunity naturally flourish, not just at home, but throughout the wider community.

Men as culture shapers

Men can help to shape a workplace where women feel valued and heard: a culture of genuine inclusion. The same goes for your personal life, where open dialogue thrives and responsibilities are shared. By embodying these principles of respect and equality within the intimacy of your home and among your friends, you contribute to broader societal change, where what is practised in private becomes the standard in public life.

Diverse teams are more innovative and perform better. Most diverse companies are now more likely than ever to outperform financially.[129] McKinsey's 2020 report shows an increasing correlation between being in the top quartile for diversity and financial outperformance.[130] It can't be denied: men who foster an inclusive environment contribute to success.

Phil talks about this in his role as CEO at AV Jennings. He recognised that confidence was an issue for some women in the workforce. His response was to introduce a 6-week course for his female employees, solely focusing on confidence building. He said while it was initially only for women in his workplace, the men also wanted to be a part of it. Today, most of his employees have completed the program and benefitted enormously.

When I asked him what more could be done from an organisational perspective, driven from the top, his response was, 'There is a lot. Equally, it really has to be a natural way of thinking and acting.' He then shared with me an example of what he meant.

Phil Kearns: action versus words alone

Phil's daughter is a talented athlete who made it to gold medal contention for the Paris 2024 Olympics. At roughly the same time, her boyfriend, also an exceptional athlete, secured a spot as a rookie player with an American pro-football team. Being a rookie player is highly competitive; you have just one season to prove yourself and make it. His first game, crucial for his career, ranking and reputation, was coming up. Instead of prioritising his game, he went

(continued)

to his coach and explained that he wanted to support his girlfriend during such a pivotal moment in her sports career. The coach, fully understanding, all but pushed him onto the plane so he could be there for her.

I was honoured that Phil shared this with me. On the surface, it might seem like an inconsequential act, but it speaks volumes and it carries significant power. It shows the younger generation supporting women, seeing and celebrating their talent, while the older generation, those in 'power positions', go beyond mere support to become true activists. By his actions the coach was helping his own player, not just Phil's daughter.

If we analyse this story even further, these actions, led by intrinsic belief patterns, occurred in what would be deemed a male-dominated industry: pro-football.

Phil is right.

We can put all the rules, policies, structures and even laws in place to 'support' women. But the work doesn't stop there. Our ongoing actions must be genuine, authentic, come from the right place and, dare I say it, from the heart.

Sexual harassment: it's still happening

If asked the question about whether sexual harassment exists at work, most men will say no. That's because you are the good guys. The horrible truth is, it is still with us. Ask a woman this question and I can pretty much guarantee the majority will have a story to tell. In fact, 85 per cent of us do![131] 'Sexual harassment is unwanted or unwelcome sexual behaviour, which makes a person feel offended, humiliated or intimidated. Sexual harassment is a type of sex discrimination.'[132]

I have been harassed in lifts, had numerous comments about my breasts, and have even been asked about my sex life. In one place where I worked, it was 'okay' for posters of naked women to be hung in the office. The poster hung behind a colleague's desk, and whoever came in could not help but avert their eyes. It was impossible not to. Try having a serious conversation with a naked magazine pullout staring down at you. Impossible.

At another place I worked, I avoided Friday night drinks. It was never pleasant: the sexual innuendos, gestures and worse that I can't really write about. Of course, because I didn't attend the drinks, I missed out on the 'bonding' and was mocked for being a 'prude'. There was always pressure to attend social events involving alcohol. Bizarrely, when I reflect, there was more pressure to drink with the team than to deliver a decent EBITDA for the divisions.

A 2018 report from the Human Rights Commission states that 23 per cent of women experienced sexual harassment at work.[133] Yet, in the *Status of Women Report Card 2024*, 6 years later, 26 per cent[134] (yes, an increase) of women who recently experienced sexual harassment experienced it at work. An even more troubling part of the report stated that 46 per cent of migrant and refugee women have experienced at least one form of sexual harassment in the workplace in the last 5 years.[135]

So, yes, I'm sorry, but you good guys need to know that sexual harassment exists. Please keep your eyes and ears peeled to see the subtle signs, which, incidentally, can include online harassment as well. New data from Australia's National Research Organisations for Women's Safety (ANROWS) shows one in seven people have used tech to sexually harass a colleague, with a quarter doing so to humiliate or frighten.[136] According to the Australian Bureau of Statistics, '26 per cent of women who experienced sexual harassment did so at work, with 57 per cent subjected to it electronically'.[137]

Here is the part where you can really help because '40 per cent of workplace sexual harassment incidents were witnessed by at least one other person'. Yet, 'in the majority of cases (69 per cent) the witness did not intervene'.[138] Please intervene. Call it out and if you are unsure if what you have seen is a form of sexual harassment, check with the person concerned.

Mentoring... and then there is sponsoring

Mentoring is one thing, but sponsorship takes it to a different level. A quote from *The New York Times* about women's career success has remained embedded in my mind, 'Mentors are good. Sponsors are better.'[139] It's simple and I love it.

Women need mentorship and I strongly advocate for women to seek out not only women but also men as mentors. Fiona Wood, Nagi Maehashi and Leila McKinnon all speak candidly about the importance of male mentors and their influences in their lives.

Leila shared how mentors were seen differently when she was coming through. 'You didn't have them so much and it was not as formal as now. Peter Harvey was someone I really looked up to and spoke about work with a great deal.' She reminisces on how fortunate she was to have that relationship and how much of an influence he had on her.

Fiona cuts straight through. For those who mentor, 'respecting potential is vitally important'. It seems the thread of identifying talent and seeing someone's potential is at the core. Phil is actively involved in the Minerva Network, a not-for-profit organisation supporting professional sportswomen. He said, 'I've been around women athletes, and I see the potential they have, what they can take with them to the business environment, and I want to help.' It was the same when I was coming through and given opportunities, so I'm trying to do that for female athletes as well now.

Sponsorship involves a more active role in advocating for the mentee's promotions and opportunities. This is especially so for employment prospects that might otherwise be out of reach. While a mentor provides advice and feedback, a sponsor can advocate on behalf of the person by leveraging their influence in the organisation, providing visibility, opening up their network or making warm introductions.[140] It's a different level of 'membership'.

Sheryl Sandberg often speaks about the men who sponsored her, helping her climb the ranks in her career. Their advocacy opened doors that might have been closed due to bias.

There are no ifs or buts about it: sponsorship makes a dramatic impact on career and earning advancements. This is a key area where men can make a difference. We appreciate the advice you give us, and we need it, but what we truly require is someone to open the door with a genuine invitation and endorsement.

Walk with us

Men's involvement is not just about offering support from the sidelines. It is about being active, vocal and fully committed partners in this journey towards gender equity. The kind of support women need is best shown through small, consistent and genuine actions that reflect one's character. Those who witness genuine change know it starts in the quiet moments, through the unspoken yet reliable understanding that binds us together.

As fathers, partners, husbands and friends, men have the opportunity to help create a world where equity is not a distant ideal but an everyday reality. In these roles, the most deeply felt support lies not in leading the charge, but in walking beside women, sharing the load and standing firm against the winds of bias. A true partnership, much like love, is built on countless small threads of respect, empathy and shared purpose.

I've always had a bit of a hero complex. I've always challenged myself personally, pushing to do better. It's not about the money for me. It's about going somewhere amazing, about proving to myself and to everyone else that I can be the hero in this story.

JULIA ROSS

Chapter 8

HARNESSING YOUR SUPPORT NETWORK

So, you have decided to make those small incremental, yet brave and meaningful decisions. Fabulous! You are also taking on board some of the false beliefs that are holding you back. Even better! You are on track to be a million dollars ahead.

But you can't do it on your own. Well ... you can, but it will be a whole lot harder, and who needs that? Chapter 8 focuses on harnessing your support network. These are the people who believe in you and see your potential. They support you in taking that vital first step and keep providing ongoing support when times get tough — because times do, and will, get hard.

Some of what I explore in chapter 8 may already be familiar to you, while other parts might catch you by surprise. As you did in chapter 6, I encourage you to be mindful in this chapter, too, of your cognitive dissonance. After all, our support network consists of those closest to us, and there might be some truths about the support we do or don't receive that can be hard to hear.

Surprising facts: truths that shouldn't be true

- According to the ABS, in Australia women spend 4.13 hours per day on unpaid domestic and care work compared to 2.14 hours for men.[141]

- Globally, 76.4 per cent of unpaid domestic work is carried out by women.[142]

- In developed countries, women take up 65 per cent of unpaid work and in emerging economies 80.2 per cent.[143]

- Those with supportive spouses are more likely to perform better at work and achieve higher earnings.[144]

- In Australia, 33 per cent of the gender pay gap is due to care and family responsibilities.[145]

Who cheers for you?

It is your birthday (literally!). A brand-spanking new baby, beautiful in every way and the apple of your parents' eyes. The obstetrician does their check: eyes, arms, beating heart and yes, potential, right there, tucked discreetly away between the brain and the heart. You go home with your parents, and your life's adventure begins.

You reach various milestones: crawling, walking, jabbering and then speaking. That's you working on your abilities, putting in the effort and striving to reach your potential. The 'failures' of falling down when you try to walk are learning opportunities to do better. You keep trying and even attempt different strategies and techniques to conquer the necessary skill of walking. Place your foot at a different angle, don't carry a bottle at the same time and attempt walking sans nappy for better weight distribution.

It doesn't feel that hard to stand up, grab the couch and start walking. You stubbornly push away your parents' help, driven by the thrill of achievement and pride—'Look at me, I did it!' Instinctively, you know to just keep going. Failure? You don't even know what it is. Sure, at times you are afraid. That is part of the course of evaluating risk, learning and acquiring knowledge. But you also have equal parts courage. Of course, the look of delight on your parents' faces and their clapping is enough encouragement and motivation for the next step and to keep going.

As we mature, the external validation is gradually replaced by an expectation of self-sufficiency and independence. The exuberant clapping and encouragement fade, and often with them go the faith and confidence in ourselves. Yet, as adults, there are times when we still need others to keep believing in us. As for women challenging the pay gap, this requirement is non-negotiable.

Ongoing support

It's not just about celebrating you; it's about being surrounded by those who are as invested in your dreams as you are. That's our inner circle.

It's impossible to close the gap, for women to be in a position to earn more, without ongoing, unremitting support, advocacy, cheering and clapping from all fronts—society as a whole—but most importantly, from our inner circle.

One of the key support areas is at home. The crucial questions are:

- Who stands in your corner?

- When you go home at night and share your wins, who jumps up and down for you?

- When the promotion or opportunity of a lifetime finally arrives, who's opening the champagne, celebrating and slapping you on the back?

- Are your supporters more excited than you? They should be.

This is where your supporters matter the most:

- What happens when the job or promotion feels overwhelming or stressful?

- Who listens and advises you when self-doubt creeps in?

- When you fear you might fail, who helps you to find the strength to keep going?

- Who's there for you when quitting feels like the easiest option?

- When balancing home responsibilities weighs heavy on you, who helps ease the burden and reminds you, 'you are not letting everyone down'?

There are those who pull you back from the brink, helping you to see perspective and reinstate your calm. They believe in you unwaveringly, offering endless encouragement and support even when you feel ready to give up.

If your supporters are invested in your dreams, they won't give up on you or allow you to give up on yourself. Your best supporters are brave enough to be honest with you, helping you to confront the hard truths and to stay on course when the path gets rocky.

They might say:

- 'Yes, the expectations are a lot right now. But does that mean quitting is the answer?'

- 'Why are you trying to be Superwoman, taking on the impossible task of being everything to everyone? No-one can.'

- 'Just because it's difficult now doesn't mean it will always be this way. Tough moments are temporary.'
- 'Maybe you need more help at home. What can I do to help lighten the load?'
- 'Maybe what is required is a reminder to "push through, stay committed, put in the work and keep striving".'
- 'You wanted this; you can do it; we just need to work out how. You will get through this.'

If you don't have one person among your family and friends who can tell you what you might not want to hear, then you may not have the right supporters. Not all our normal cheer squad are good in these situations. And that's okay.

In everyday situations, they are your tribe. They just might not be cut out to provide the level of support, encouragement, honesty and feedback needed to get you where you need to go. Or they may care too much and aren't able to separate their instinct to protect. You can't blame them for that. So, when seeking advice or help, be careful who you choose and what story you tell. Make sure it's truthful and balanced and take responsibility for your part in the issue. If you need them to be objective—and you do—then you must also be objective.

Which brings me to you ...

Are you supporting or sabotaging yourself?

Maybe it's you. Maybe you make it too hard for those who care about you to play their support role. Are you 'hard work' and do you become defensive when the people you love and respect share what they see as the truth? Accepting their feedback might cause you to confront uncomfortable truths and if these discussions regularly end in an argument, that might be one reason.

EARNING POWER

If receiving the truth is a challenge, then, logically, we will gravitate towards people who confirm our blind spots and illusions, and entertain our victimhood.

I say this with hesitation. Sometimes, people get used to surrounding themselves with 'yes' people because they want attention and to remain vulnerable. There is a certain power that comes with this, mainly because it provides an excuse not to change or take responsibility.

Some feedback that might be hard to hear:

- If you are thinking of quitting, how long have you really tried coping with the job? If it's 6 months or less, that might not be long enough.

- Do you need assistance at home or at work? If you can identify the need, have you asked for help?

- Are you struggling with self-doubt or the workload? Both can be addressed, by the way!

- Have you shared your struggles with someone at work —maybe your manager or co-workers? Sometimes when we voice our concerns, it can lead to unexpected support.

- Is the issue you have with the job itself, or do you perhaps feel an overall unhappiness with life or yourself? (It happens.) Understanding the core issue might really help you make the right decision.

- Are you realistic with your expectations, or perhaps trying to meet impossible standards?

Protecting our self-esteem is important, but it's also essential to confront reality.

Don't be resistant to hearing feedback and others' viewpoints. Be the person who is open and welcoming of it. Be Oliver and ask for 'more please'. Honest feedback should always be seen as a 'gift' offered by those who put our interests first, challenging our illusions and encouraging our growth, even when it causes us—and them—discomfort.

The non-supporters

Yes, they are also known as toxic friends. If we are lucky, we have friends who build us up. Sometimes we also have friends who hold us back. Toxic 'friends' will typically dismiss your feelings or emotions, won't have your best interests at heart, will envy your success or perceived success, and won't be happy for your achievements, but will be delighted when it looks like you might fail.

This is when they seem the most interested in hearing your woes. Incidentally, dangerously, these can be work 'friends' as well.

Amid challenging times, it can be hard to distinguish the toxic from the genuine supporters. Toxic 'friends' flourish when they control and manipulate others, meaning you. They often carry deep insecurities within themselves, no matter the confidence they portray. Because of that, they tend to project their fears and insecurities onto those around them. This doesn't excuse their actions, but reminds us that labelling someone as 'toxic' is rarely the full story, indicating deeper struggles they may not even fully understand. It's no wonder that, to maintain their perceived strength or overconfidence, they are at their 'best' (which is really their worst!) when you feel small or weak. If you are exposed to toxic behaviour over a longer period, it easily provokes doubt, questions your self-esteem and confidence and impacts your decisions.

Spotting the signs early and defining better boundaries is essential.

To identify your toxic 'friends' ask yourself:

- Do they ever challenge your negative mantra?

- Will they offer a positive viewpoint to your pessimistic one?

- Do they encourage you to quit, give up and not put your hand up without offering any solutions?

- Do they add salt to your wounds by reminding you of previous grievances just to pull you down?

- Do they undermine your confidence by subtly questioning your abilities or decisions?

- Do they compete with you rather than celebrate your successes, turning everything into a comparison?

Here is Fiona Wood's upfront voice on the importance of having the right people around you.

Professor Fiona Wood: 'I was connecting with the positive and shimmying on through'

In my discussion with Fiona Wood, she made it clear that having the right people in your life is essential.

Fiona starts with reflections on her childhood. Fiona's parents had such a positive influence on her with regard to their view on work, believing in 'hard work', 'the enjoyment of work' and the wonderful feeling of a 'job well done'. She was also brought up in a supportive family environment to believe she could 'achieve anything' if she was prepared to work for it. Her upbringing also emphasised 'making sure I didn't waste my energy on the negative. Instead, I was connecting with the positive and shimmying on through'.

In the workforce, she talks openly about the barriers, but equally of those who supported her. 'I had many senior clinicians tell me that surgery wasn't a job for women, but I also had those who supported me: colleagues, senior colleagues.'

> This mixture of discouragement and support made it clear to her that while others' judgements and biases could hinder progress, it's ultimately up to you to decide what to listen to: 'There are many people who will tell you what you "can't". It's their frame of reference, their judgement. You don't have to listen to them.'
>
> A main theme that comes through in my talk with Fiona is that of 'potential'. It was so strongly emphasised when we spoke that it feels almost like sacred ground. Here is what she said when discussing mentors: 'Those that respect your potential are so vitally important.' The sentiment was similar for life partners and husbands: 'To settle for someone who doesn't respect your potential is a danger.'
>
> Fiona remarked, 'Respect for your ambitions is not negotiable. Don't compromise your dreams for anyone who won't support them.'
>
> When it comes to family, she reflected, 'It's about finding something that is a successful collaboration with your partner.' When Fiona talks about this part of her life, she isn't afraid to admit that she was 'more hands-on with the children, absolutely'. It is very clear, though, that it was Fiona's choice. She constantly refers to it as a collaboration and 'making it work'. Having a successful collaboration and the right people around you doesn't have to mean 50/50. It's what works for you.

In the work environment, Fiona emphasises, most importantly, 'Don't forget to be a supporter of those behind you. Pay it forward.'

It's clear Fiona chooses the people to be around, understanding all too well also the importance of ignoring the noise. Fiona's life and career have been proof of how valuable and crucial it is to surround yourself with the right people.

Partner support

If you have a partner, they can be the most influential and important person in your life.

According to research from Washington University, when it comes to raises, promotions and other measures of career success, it's the husband or wife who may exert the biggest influence on workplace performance. The study indicated that those with supportive partners, regardless of gender, are more likely to reduce stress, provide emotional stability and encourage risk-taking in one's career—all factors that contribute to higher income.[146]

This makes sense, common sense in fact. Yet, husbands with much higher incomes than their wives have a lower chance of divorcing, and evidence shows that marriages are less stable when the wife outearns the husband.[147]

A separate study by the University of Chicago concludes that 'many relationships that do not conform to the traditional norm of the man playing the role of the provider do not fare well, with those marriages being 50 per cent more likely to end in divorce'.[148] Deep down, we knew it to be true.

Women still face the complexities of outperforming their partners. This reality can be uncomfortable to acknowledge and a challenge to discuss openly. From my experience of placing women in jobs, I have seen these scenarios occur regularly and it became a strong impetus behind writing this book.

It's not just earnings outperformance, it's also in areas such as furthering education, career advancements and, sadly, when women show high engagement in their jobs and working environment. On the surface, their partners seem threatened. I am unsure if it is because the home and domestic responsibilities are not the centre of their partners' lives, or something else. Why do they have to be mutually exclusive? It is healthy for all of us to have a sense of purpose and a connection to our work.

I appreciate many of you might not find it easy to consider this in your own experience. None of us do. Yet data, research and my 30-plus years of workplace observations back it up.

It may be your spouse's issue, or maybe it's also your issue. Tensions exist on both sides: the co-contribution of your internalised beliefs that outearning your partner or having a career or financial success should be secondary to being a caregiver or nurturer. You could feel uncomfortable outearning your partner, destabilising the expected dynamic. It's not just the inferred and self-imposed pressure women have. It's society's unrelenting stronghold on men of the deep-seated beliefs about the role they, too, should be playing.

If you're reading this and find it difficult to relate, that's entirely valid. Relationships come in many forms and the dynamics vary widely. Yet the studies and research offer important insights and they shouldn't be dismissed just because they don't pertain to your circumstances.

Or do they? Be mindful of cognitive dissonance, the mental tug-of-war that happens when we sympathise with others yet quickly dismiss these insights as irrelevant to our own lives. It's worth considering whether what seems distant might, in fact, reflect subtler dynamics in your own experience.

For a moment, let's revisit the story from chapter 5 about Silvia. Her situation could be any of thousands of similar stories. The opportunity to earn and learn more, realise professional goals and personal dreams for herself and her family. Not forgetting, the opportunity was presented to Silvia by her boss, an external source of support who believes in her potential. Here's what happened next.

Silvia happily accepted the opportunity. The hours increased at work (from 4 days to 5), as did the pressure and workload. It's all very normal when taking on a new role, let alone a step up. While Silvia's workload at work increased, it did not decrease at the other end — at home — where the expectation was still to do all that was being done before. The daycare drop-offs, pick-ups and first point of call for any family issues (including elderly parental issues) and domestic responsibilities remained.

There was little understanding or support from her partner, who viewed it as solely her decision. This sentiment was echoed by both sides of the family — parents, in-laws, siblings — who questioned, 'Why wasn't she fulfilling her motherhood responsibilities?' and 'Why have children if you aren't there for them?'

Let's fast forward to 6 months later.

Silvia stayed in the job for 6 months before quitting. Faced with overwhelming external pressures and internal doubts, the strain became unbearable. She was so crushed and depleted of confidence she couldn't even stick out the agreed 12 months. Silvia didn't ask her boss for help or to return to her old job.

Silvia was never going to be successful in the new role and close her earnings gap without adequate support from home. Had Silvia stuck with the job, I am confident she would have been successful. With more experience and knowledge, she might have developed a rhythm and way of working that balanced better with other aspects of her life. Achieving this would have required time, some sacrifices and, importantly, partner support.

I have little doubt that if Silvia had kept going, she might have earned that extra million dollars over her lifetime. As for whether suddenly earning more than her partner affected the household dynamic, I can't be certain, but I suspect so.

Figure 8.1 and figure 8.2 (overleaf) show three different potential earnings and financial scenarios over Silvia's lifetime:

1. *Solid grey line:* Silvia sticks with the new role, continues earning $130 000 and applies minimum wage growth of 2.4 per cent every two years

2. *Dotted line:* Silvia sticks with the new role, continues earning $130 000 and applies minimum wage growth of 2.4 per cent every two years. She takes one year off in two years for her second child and returns to work 4 days a week thereafter

3. *Solid black line:* Silvia returns to her old job, paying $80 000 per year, applies minimum wage growth every two years.

Additionally, and importantly, the figures also show the impact on superannuation accrual.

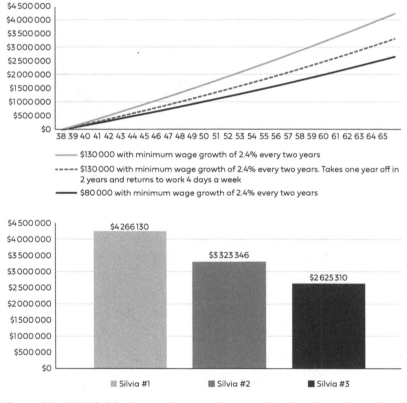

Figure 8.1: Silvia's lifetime salary earnings projection based on the three different financial scenarios

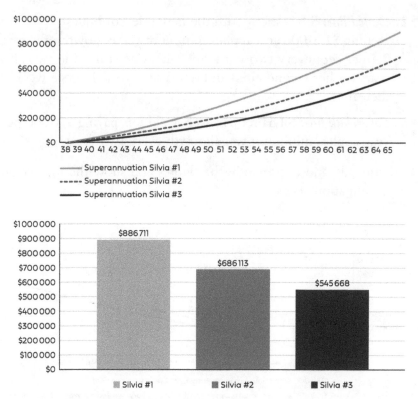

Figures 8.2: Silvia's accumulated superannuation earnings projection based on the three different financial scenarios

I wonder if Silvia or her family realised the full financial ramifications of her decision. The information could have provided additional motivation and consideration and perhaps life might not have appeared quite so overwhelming for all parties. Crucially, how important was this opportunity to Silvia? That answer determines the level of support and effort.

If the roles were reversed and the opportunity to advance in career and earnings fell into her partner's lap, what level of support would he have expected and received? Where might he be now? I'm pretty sure we all know the answer.

Which brings me to the all-important question: *What's love got to do with it?* Everything. This time I'm not referring to our partners, family or inner circle. It's your self-love.

Self-love: you support you

Self-love isn't about making time for massages. Nice as they might be, if you have an abundance of self-love, you may never need another massage in your lifetime. Read on to see Julia Ross's perspective.

You may recall from chapter 1, Julia talking about being interviewed on television and almost being shamed about whether she did 'tuck shop' or not. The (female) journalist loaded the anti-feminist gun and took aim, asking provocatively (not supportively), 'Do you do tuckshop?'

Assuredly, backing herself, Julia deflected the bullet, stating, 'No, I don't do tuck.' Own the choices we make and the rights we have to make these choices. It is a healthy part of self-love.

> *I don't do tuck.*
>
> *I couldn't have built the business if I wasn't aggressive. It was appropriate for the time.*
>
> *I'm wired like that. I would have made a very good warrior. I keep going.*
> **Julia Ross**

On this point, as a temperature check, I am sure we all think we have progressed since those days. Hmm... In the 1990s, that question would never have been posed to a man. Fast track to today, and when we ask a male such a question, it is usually a staged set-up. Because — what a surprise — the answer is 'Yes, I do tuck shop.' He gets Father of the Year and a fanfare.

For centuries, women have been putting others' interests ahead of their own. I am not suggesting we go rogue and become grossly selfish, abscond all responsibilities and suddenly pursue a hedonistic life. That's not going to work either. It's not sustainable, nor would it be fulfilling. Equally, when we care and love for our family and those who mean the most to us, it's understandable that we make them a priority.

It feels good, right? I don't know about you, but the joy of doing something nice for those you love, even if it means putting yourself out, is hard to beat. It is usually not seen as a sacrifice and not so much a chore as a pleasure. It is what makes us human, gives us connection and provides that all-important factor we simply can't live without: love.

What about self-love? It is the essential ingredient for self-esteem and self-worth. Self-love is the internal love and care for ourselves. Self-love serves as the basis from which all other forms of love originate. Without it, the love we give to others can't be complete. To be balanced and authentic in our relationships, we must first nurture deep respect and care for ourselves.

It's a delicate balance though, when we devote much of ourselves to others. Our needs, wants and priorities could become secondary. Although, to be honest, if only we were second. Many women fall in well after everyone else: family, children, partner, parents, dog, cat and rabbits.

If you don't truly believe what I am saying, perhaps pause and take note over the next few weeks:

- Whose gym or yoga session gets cancelled (or maybe you stopped those classes years ago)?

- What about the hair or doctor's appointment that gets cancelled so many times they threaten to cancel you?

- Who gets the last biscuit, slice of cake and milk?

- Who leaves work early (again) to run to the childcare/ school/family emergency?

- Who stays home with the sick child?

- Who drops everything to attend to an elderly parent?

- Who works part-time to cater to family responsibilities?

- Who puts on hold their needs 'to get my children through school'?

And here are a few more:

- Whose car has all the family trappings—baby seats, soccer gear, muddy boots and netballs—and hasn't been cleaned since you got it?

- What about the daily walk you committed to or the catch-ups with friends? How frequently are they postponed?

- What about the event—school, work or social—that you force yourself to attend because it's 'the right thing to do'? Even though you can barely keep your eyes open—and, truth be known, you don't want to go.

- Who has no energy to do what you might have wanted to do anyway? An extra hour of sleep becomes the best birthday or Mother's Day gift.

These may seem like small, inconsequential details, and if you are like me, you might say, 'But I want to, I'm happy to' or at least, 'Most of the time, I am happy to, and it's just life anyway—we are all in the same boat.'

Ah, but we are not. Women carry the overwhelming burden of working and managing the home, caring, family and domestic responsibilities and putting themselves right at the end of the priority list.

While I say all this, and I know it rings true for many women, we should still mention that things are changing in many households. There are men out there taking on these roles, and many families are figuring out how to redefine sharing. Still, those old-school expectations hang around for many women.

So, when we turn our attention to the workforce, how do women miraculously change suit, put themselves first and confidently assert value in a professional workplace setting to bridge the pay gap? Fraught with contradictions, it's a Jekyll and Hyde jump. Consequently, the question of self-love becomes crucial here: how can a woman truly love and value herself if she remains financially dependent on others or feels unworthy of financial success? As we have established, financial independence is key not just for security but also for empowerment.

Not surprisingly, research in behavioural economics has uncovered that our relationship with money is deeply tied to our sense of self-worth. One study by Dr Kathleen Vohs, a psychologist at the University of Minnesota, shows that thinking about money, or what she refers to as 'money priming', can induce feelings of independence and autonomy.[149] This scientific research shows how love, money and self-worth are connected and can significantly influence our behaviour and mindset.

The outcome suggested that being financially independent is not just about having money but is also supported by increased self-sufficiency and confidence, which are essential to self-love. In addition, when women perceive themselves as financially capable and independent, they are more likely to act as equals in relationships.

So, there is nothing wrong with putting yourself first—and not just occasionally, but often.

Kristina Karlsson emphasises the importance of self-love and self-care and says it is 'probably the most frequent question I get asked now'. She tells me her focus on ensuring time for herself started when she had young children and was running her business. She says it was a challenging time. 'I wasn't sleeping well, so I decided then I had to look after my health.'

This was the time she started to put firm boundaries in place about what she would say 'yes' and 'no' to. She goes on to say, 'I'm an introvert so for me to have space for myself is important. I know I need it to be a better person. That's how I see it. I am a better partner, a better mum for sure and I'm also much better for the business.'

Kristina tells me that she spends two hours on her morning ritual. She also admits, 'I know that's not a possibility for everyone.'

Here is Kristina's daily ritual:

I go to bed early.

I get up early.

I walk every morning—you see the world differently.

I journal every morning—usually three pages—whatever is in my head. Or it might be all the things I am grateful for.

I meditate (if you can't meditate, sit in silence for just 5 minutes).

It's good to get a connection with yourself and see something that perhaps is much bigger than you. I don't think it's selfish. It's actually an investment in yourself.

Kristina's final point on self-love and her morning ritual is, 'I mean, I say [I do it] every morning, but I'm human and I do miss it every now and then ... but hardly [ever]'.

When we prioritise ourselves, we do it not only to create the necessary moments of pleasure or even solitude, but also to recognise the crucial role that self-nourishment plays in all our relationship arenas. We open ourselves to examine honestly and reflect upon the habits of our 'yesses' and 'nos'—and figure out where they come from. We see if our responses and behaviours come from our fear of rejection or disapproval, or from a more positive place.

When we say 'no', we create space to say 'yes' to all those things that matter. If you are saying 'yes' a lot purely out of obligation, consider saying 'no'. Sometimes there is strength, self-worth and an abundance of self-love in saying no. If those around you are your supporters, they will understand, and if not, tough. It's your choice and your decision—own it and remember, 'I don't do tuck.'

External support: networking and mentoring

Men network exceptionally well. It seems as natural to them as walking, breathing and sleeping. They don't make it look hard, intimidating or awkward. As women, we should take note. It's the same with mentors: men seem to have them in every pocket. In my interview with Leila McKinnon, she mentions this as a key difference and observes that men often have groups of men who look out for each other, back each other up and support each other.

It's a sad reality that most women don't have mentors, and the thought of networking is abhorrent to us. If you don't have a 'someone', welcome to the club. According to one global study, women don't actively seek out mentors and 63 per cent of women have never had a formal mentor.[150] When we do, for official mentorships, 75 per cent of women prefer a female mentor, and for spontaneous mentoring, 80.5 per cent prefer a female.[151]

This can be very problematic, not just in terms of access to women in a position to provide mentorship but also our own potential for all realms of bias. We should be seeking out men and women as mentors, officially and spontaneously. They provide a different perspective, and, after all, if men hold most leadership and executive positions, they are in 'the know'. Phil Kearns echoes this point to me, saying, 'Men hold a lot of the roles at the top — we've established that, so use us!'

It provides access and pathways, but additionally, and importantly, increases the broader understanding of the issues women face in the workplace. Keeping it contained to just women might garner compassion and understanding, but we need more than that; we need action. Additionally, men seeking out mentoring from female leaders is also advantageous. So go out and proactively find a mentor — and don't discount male ones. They could be your biggest advocatory.

Leila admitted that networking as a concept felt odd as well. This is her approach and I love it for its simplicity and authenticity.

If I am not learning anything, then I'll look to ways to improve and learn something new. So, if I'd been working in the newsroom, I would think, I don't really know anybody over at A Current Affair. Maybe if I introduce myself and start talking to people, I'll develop other contacts. The more people you have good relationships with — and if you have always been reliable and able to perform to their expectations — the more your name will come up. I sort of don't think of it as cynically as networking, but it sort of is, I suppose, as you have a great network of relationships.

Fiona spoke of one of her main mentors, Dr Harold McComb, saying,

We didn't view it as mentoring then as we do now. When I look back now with the current lens, that level of support was earned. It wasn't like now, where you ask for someone to mentor you. [Rather,] it was me asking, 'May I come into the operating room? May I learn from you?' Then I'm there, and I'm learning. By working hard and demonstrating that in your work, people either support you or not. Having someone like that who respects your potential is vitally important.

Kristina says, 'Mentors have been so important to me.' The way she went about seeking out mentors was to pinpoint the areas in which she needed knowledge, find those people and have 'loads and loads of coffees'. 'I think, okay, who has done this before me? Who can I learn from? People love to help.'

Reflecting on the power of mentorship, Peta shared with me the support she received when she first started working in politics. 'I noticed there were only about five or six staffers across the Howard era who were the experts and when they were in the room or the chamber, everyone would come to them and want their view on difficult matters of policy or procedure. I thought, "well that's one way to be a valuable staffing asset—become someone who does the hard-yards and builds up expertise". The harder or more unpopular the area was, such as senate procedure which is notoriously arcane, the better.' So, over the years, to learn as much as she could from these people, she asked every question she could think of. Her boss encouraged her to reach out to a particular female deputy clerk, who was highly knowledgeable and skilled. Peta said, 'I used to spend every Friday with her as a junior staffer. This carried on for the 16 years I was in politics' she said proudly, recalling how she became a self-confessed, 'senate procedural boffin'.

For all of us, but particularly women, embracing and cultivating strong, supportive relationships can be a powerful tool in overcoming societal barriers and gaining financial independence.

We need more Gail Kellys.

JULIA ROSS

Chapter 9

TOOLS AND TIPS FROM DREAM ACHIEVERS

Financial freedom and independence are key to bridging the gender pay gap. So too are the journey of self-actualisation and the innate power of self-belief that accompanies it. Having faith in oneself is the catalyst for taking action, pursuing opportunities and advocating for one's value. And it's needed to realise our dreams.

The tools and tips in chapter 9 come from dream achievers: the talented, extraordinary and inspiring women I interviewed. Each of these women chose to take control of their destiny and define their own values. These are not women who waited for permission or validation. They claimed their space. This last chapter shares more of their advice and wisdom for you to claim your space too.

Wisdom isn't just having experience: it's the development of a deeper understanding of the world. It requires self-awareness, compassion, mindfulness, patience, and an open and questioning mind. Wisdom isn't a given either. Reaching 'the top', being successful, mature—or old for that matter—doesn't mean you have wisdom. It takes a rare and open mind to cultivate wisdom.

Before the accolades and achievement is the work. These women shared a path similar to that of many others—one of wins and setbacks, obstacles, chances taken and lost. So, if you find yourself thinking, like in chapter 6, 'It's okay for them'... it wasn't. Their successes were not handed to them, except for one incredible gift: they grew up believing they could achieve whatever they wanted in life!

Chapter 9 delves into dreams, SWOT analysis, passion and 'finding your voice'. Let's start with our dreams...

Amazing facts about amazing women

- Julia Ross became the first and only single-owned female company CEO to list on the Australian Stock Exchange (I believe at the time it was also a global record, but who's counting).

- Nagi Maehashi's first cookbook, *Dinner*, launched in 2022, is the fastest-selling cookbook in Australian publishing history. Not to be outdone, Nagi's second book, *Tonight* has broken the record of the highest first week sales for a Non-Fiction title since BookScan Australia records began in December 2002.

- Professor Fiona Wood's enduring legacy is her work with co-inventor Marie Stoner pioneering the innovative 'spray-on skin' technique (ReCell). Today the technique is used worldwide.

- Leila McKinnon has interviewed seven Australian prime ministers and Beyoncé (twice!).

- Kristina Karlsson was the founder of kikki.K, a business with 1500 employees, an online store serving over 150 countries and a total revenue of $650 million.

- Peta Credlin is one of the longest serving chiefs of staff to a national leader in Australia and the longest serving female chief of staff to a prime minister.

How did they do it? Well, in this chapter we'll discover the tools and tips that helped these incredible women realise their success.

Follow your dreams

> *Sometimes, to achieve your dreams, you've just got to be brave and take the plunge.*
> **Nagi Maehashi**

> *What one action did you take today towards your dream life?*
> **Kristina Karlsson**

> *I guess I was a particular female. I was never giving up my dream for anyone.*
> **Julia Ross**

Before any journey comes the dream, the flicker of possibility that sets everything in motion. Sylvia Plath's fig tree in chapter 6 explores life's options and dreams with the message that 'everything is on offer'. To dream can mean having a particular goal — 'to be a surgeon' — or it can be an overarching aspiration: 'to live by the beach'.

When I interview people, or provide coaching and mentoring, I always ask, 'What are your aspirations?' I also follow up with, 'And what were they when you were younger?' The answers often reveal a lot, shedding light on forgotten ambitions and untapped talents. Dreaming is more than imagining future possibilities: it's about connecting with what truly motivates and drives you, and understanding how those ambitions evolve over time.

But, let's not confuse dreaming with wishful thinking. The dreams I refer to, life dreams of real possibilities, are anything but that. Wishful thinking is passive; it's hoping for an outcome without putting in the work and effort, or creating a pathway to achieve it. It's the belief that success might just 'happen' to us.

Dreams are also not trivial thoughts; they are the blueprints for creating a life of fulfilment and purpose. Here is the crucial part: to hold a dream — to see all that life can offer — requires more than just imagination. It demands intention, courage and an openness to possibilities.

Real dreams and aspirations are active and intentional. They require a clear vision paired with the willingness to invest time and effort and even face failure in pursuit of that vision. Dreams are not realised by us simply 'wanting' something to happen.

Reaching your dreams is about planning, enduring the challenges and remaining resilient in the face of setbacks. They are also a way to reframe reality by setting a direction for your actions, choices and efforts. At the same time, be cognisant of working within life's constraints because life will present us with certain unchangeable facts. Harnessed with the right mindset, these limitations help to guide us to alternative pathways.

Dreams, in their true form, are both grounded and infused with a sense of possibility. It's a delicate balance, embracing the possibility of something greater without losing sight of the steps and effort required to get there.

Dreaming means understanding the landscape of your current life and envisioning something more ... much more. This is not a fantasy but a deeply personal possibility that aligns with your values, talents and, of course, hard work. Your dreams won't come to life without intent and effort, whether that means gaining new skills, seeking mentorship or finding allies who will champion your vision.

Dreams are the starting point for personal transformation. With purpose and persistence, even the most profound internal barriers — like self-doubt or feelings of inadequacy — can be overcome.

Nagi Maehashi talks a lot about the importance of dreams. She says,

> I remember thinking in my 20s that I really wanted to put my hard work and energy into something else, something for myself. I always had that at the back of mind; it kept me going through those really rough patches at work and the long hours.

For Nagi, the dream wasn't just about starting RecipeTin Eats. It was about creating a life for herself by the beach, a dream she had nurtured for years before seizing the moment. Here is Nagi's take on dreams.

Nagi Maehashi: 'I'm not afraid to dream big. I've always had it in me'

Nagi tells me how one day, out of the blue she decided to go to the northern beaches of New South Wales for a walk along the cliffs. She said, 'I didn't even live there then, but had always loved the thought of it.'

She continues, 'I came across this small, rundown, old beach house, and it was for sale. I could see it was empty, so I snuck around the back. I know I shouldn't have! I saw it had 180 degrees of ocean views. It was way too expensive for me, but then I thought, "I'll try another way."'

Nagi tells me how she reached out to the owner and he agreed to rent it to Nagi cheaply because it was 'so rundown'. She says that she moved in a week later and fell in love with the lifestyle that she had only ever imagined before.

Then, this is where RecipeTin Eats comes in. Nagi explained that she tried the commute to work for 3 months. But it was too much. That was the instigator for the next part of her dream. Nagi said to me, determinedly, 'I wasn't willing to give up my lifestyle, so I thought, this was the time I should try something for myself. I thought, if not now, then when?'

Ta da...RecipeTin Eats was founded. 'Sometimes, to achieve your dreams, you've just got to be brave and take the plunge.'

As Nagi talks casually about these pivotal moments in her life, they might seem impulsive ... but don't be fooled. They were well thought out. As mentioned in Chapter 5, Nagi conducted a SWOT analysis of her skills and identified the new ones she needed to develop. She had also been saving all these years, always keeping in mind her ultimate goal of doing something for herself.

The foresight in savings provided Nagi with the ability to start on the way to realising her goal, but also acted as a 'security' for those times of immense struggles and self-doubt. During those trying times, it can be tempting to give up. Having the backup of financial security helped Nagi stay focused and resist the temptation and lure to give up.

Now Nagi is an international success story. She has billions of visits to her website, millions of followers on social media, and a global fan base from pretty much every corner and country in the world. She has also set up a charity called RecipeTin Meals, because 'no-one should go hungry'.

SWOT analysis: making your dream a reality

Let's look at a SWOT analysis, just like Nagi did, to chart the course towards making your dream a reality.

SWOT is a tool traditionally used in business strategy. It stands for Strengths, Weaknesses, Opportunities and Threats. The strengths and weaknesses are internal factors, and the opportunities and threats are viewed as external factors. A SWOT can make the unknown known, to highlight a clear path forward. Displaying the threats and weaknesses is like 'Siri' saying, 'Watch out, this is where you could stumble.' It helps you identify the areas that need attention, allowing you to adapt and find new ways to keep moving towards your dream.

Let's take Silvia (in chapter 5) as an example. If her dream was to be successful in her new role as a sales agent, she would have overlaid the SWOT with the job, home requirements and her capabilities.

This is how the steps of a SWOT analysis might have looked for Silvia:

- *Step 1:* List job requirements: sales and networking abilities, real-estate experience (ideally as an agent), understanding of industry terminology, good written and verbal communication, people skills, resilience, EQ, negotiation skills, work 5 days a week (including Saturday).

- *Step 2:* List personal and professional capabilities: strong administration, organisational skills, leadership (from team and office management), problem-solving, technological proficiency, and good written and verbal communication.

- *Step 3:* Evaluate the job requirement versus the personal capabilities.

Here's how to perform your own SWOT analysis:

- *Strengths:* List the skills, experiences, transferable skills and qualities that align with the job requirements. Include feedback and attributes others such as your manager has shared with you.

- *Weaknesses:* List the areas that fall short of the job requirements, including those you don't fully meet. Be honest about areas where you lack experience or knowledge, as putting your head in the sand won't help you. Use feedback you have received from others such as your manager. For Sylvia, these might be sales and networking abilities, real-estate experience as an agent and, ideally, working 5 days a week (including Saturday).

- *Opportunities:* List aspects of the job that provide benefits: career, money, financial freedom, securing your family's future, professional and personal growth. Make sure to focus on the benefits that align with your needs.

- *Threats:* External factors that could hinder your chances of success, including any personal circumstances that might impact your ability to perform the job. In Syvia's case, these are personal circumstances, home and domestic demands.

Conducting a SWOT like this on a new and potentially demanding role provides awareness for pain points that might not have been so visible before. Mostly, like it did for Nagi, it gives an opportunity to find a solution and plan for any gaps that may be present.

When you do a SWOT, it helps you to make more confident and calculated decisions and achieve those dreams!

You need passion

Throughout my interviews with the wonderful women featured in this book, common threads often emerged. Passion is one of them.

> *When I'm passionate about what I am doing I can work so much harder.*
> **Kristina Karlsson**

Just like Kristina, Nagi Maehashi speaks about the importance of passion in work. In her words,

> *You've got to have passion for what you are doing. Not just the skill, but passion as well. Because if you don't have the passion, you will never have the drive.*

She laughs as she reflects on her career choices, saying, 'That's why I'm not a stockbroker. Sure, I have the finance skills, and the money would be great, but I have no passion for it.'

Kristina shares a similar philosophy. She explained to me how passion is closely tied to your dreams and goals. She said to me,

> *I have found when I am passionate about what I am doing, I work so much harder towards my goals. It has also meant I cope better with the hard work as well.*

The link between passion and achieving success or personal goals cannot be overstated. Time again, I've seen how passion is one of the key drivers behind the successful people I meet. It's one of the outlying and distinguishing factors that fuels ambition.

Passion not only drives individuals to pursue their goals but also influences how others perceive and support them. Research attributes the positive effects of passion on professional success to intrapersonal characteristics. It proposes that intrapersonal processes are critical because observers confer status on and support those who express passion. Or as I like to put it, 'passion is contagious!'

Yet, frequently during interviews, I encounter women who tell me they are no longer passionate about their work. Sometimes the perceived lack of passion is just boredom. However, from my experience, more often the loss of passion stems from neglect. When we stop paying attention or investing in our work or careers, it's inevitable the excitement fades. Passion requires nurturing; even the most fulfilling job can start to feel routine without it.

I'm not immune to this either. At different points in my career, I've been there too. In some ways, it is bound to happen. As we go through life, we juggle and prioritise what is typically most urgent, but not what is necessarily most important. I have discovered, with only 24 hours in the day (what happened to the other 12 I so desperately need!), something has to give. As we covered in the previous chapter, this is why self-love so vital.

When we first enter the workforce, its demands are unrelenting: learning, development, skills acquisition, curiosity and more. Is it any wonder being so immersed, we are so motivated, excited and passionate. As we progress, we can afford to take our foot off the pedal... a bit. We can even, on occasion, use work hacks to get us by. However, if we allow these to continue to the point that they become habits, our passion naturally takes a detour. Passion needs nourishment.

Just like our romantic relationships, if you want passion to remain, it needs attention and investment. When left unattended for too long, it gets harder to reignite and requires serious effort and commitment. However, with intention and care, passion can be revived and even deepened.

Having a passion for what you do is connected to a growth mindset. It encourages perseverance and resilience. And believe it or not, we can be passionate and motivated even with the most menial of tasks ... if we approach them with the right mindset and curiosity.

Nagi recalls the early days of her career, saying,

I did a lot of filing and photocopying—you know, boring stuff. But I was always learning something from it. Sounds strange, learning from photocopying, I know. But you do. Do 500 copies, and you are learning. It's also about the work ethic, caring for the team and not letting them down, and it's character building. So, yeah, you can learn from things like this. People don't realise it, though.

Passion isn't just about grand ambitions or fiery enthusiasm. It is also in our daily work, the growth and commitment to doing things well, even with the smallest of tasks. Nagi's story shows us that passion can be cultivated through learning and caring about the impact you make, no matter how menial the task. Ultimately, passion is a choice we make every day, in every action.

This leads me to the importance of continuous learning.

Continuous learning

A mindset of continuous learning is imperative. It keeps you current, on your toes, relevant, present and observant, and helps you build confidence. It's also an important life skill. For Leila McKinnon, this commitment to self-improvement is a defining aspect of her career.

It connects directly to her sense of professionalism and pride in doing a good job. Learning and improvement are not just tasks, but core motivations that drive her forward.

Here is Leila's approach to learning and her career.

Leila McKinnon: 'I do a lot of listening'

Leila shares an early memory about a story she did on the Melbourne Cup. 'I only had a short amount of time to work on the story. I reviewed it and could see I didn't get the right emotion across. But there was no time to change it. My boss saw it and said, "What happened?" I said, "I don't know. I'm sorry, I just messed it up. I won't do it again."'

This candid moment shows how accepting mistakes and learning from them was something Leila embraced from the beginning. 'I think I was quite good at facing up to mistakes, apologising and learning from them.'

She goes on to say, 'I think I'm a big critic of myself and sometimes I drive myself mad analysing and thinking what I could have done better today. It does put pressure on you, but it's good for self-awareness too.'

Leila's approach to learning remains steadfast, even as a seasoned journalist. Reflecting on her work at the Paris 2024 Olympics, she says, 'Well, I was aware of any little mistakes that I made. Sometimes they weren't even my mistake; somebody might have said something incorrectly in my ear, as part of the broadcast, and I'd end up floundering a bit. I always think how could I have done that better? If I don't think like that, then I'm not doing my best job.'

Her commitment to self-improvement is evident in her process of review and feedback. 'I'll watch it afterwards and most of the time think, *That was good, and that really worked*. But if it doesn't, I think, *How can I fix that?*' She said, laughing, to me, 'I mean I might make it look like I'm cruising, but the whole time I'm policing everything.'

(continued)

> Learning is not just about accumulating knowledge. Sometimes, it's about unlearning habits. Leila shares her experience of transitioning from a formal news reporter to a more relaxed presenter. 'When I did the *Today* show, I was the formal news reporter, a credible and informative journalist. That was my primary training. When I went to *Weekend Today*, it took me a long time to break out of that.'
>
> Her executive producer gave her valuable feedback. 'People have had enough of Leila McKinnon. We want to see Leila.' Leila shared with me, 'You know, you don't even know you're doing it. I was grateful for the advice. So, you've got to unlearn things and learn new things.'
>
> Even though Leila has spent most of her career in the same organisation, she's embraced the challenge of different roles, from investigative journalist to hosting *State of Origin* and even *Ninja Warrior*, all while continuing to grow. 'I think it's good to experience different things. I am always looking to learn something more or achieve something different all the time. If I'm not learning, then I'll look for another role to challenge myself so that I'm always improving.'

Leila's journey shows that learning is not a finite goal but an ongoing process that requires humility, resilience and adaptability. At times it seems Leila's approach is a deep engagement with the unknown, where curiosity becomes the driver for self-improvement and where self-reflection allows for growth even after the most challenging of experiences.

Peta Credlin's approach to learning is equally committed and tenacious.

Peta Credlin: 'Like Hugh Jackman, be a triple threat'

In theatre, a triple threat is a multi-talented and well-rounded performer, so called because they can sing, dance and act. Peta's version of a triple threat is less about the singing, dancing and acting but most certainly about being multi-skilled and talented. Referring to her role in politics she says it was about, 'knowing your specific policy remit but also economics and budget matters, procedure and political language'. She explains, 'just because you're not the person carrying the legislation, that doesn't mean you don't need to learn the language.'

Her advice to women on being a triple threat is direct, 'I would say to women in politics, "'if you are not comfortable with the narrative of your portfolio, learn it rapidly."' Peta highlights to me that a 'good two thirds of the government portfolios have a heavy financial basis so if that's not your forte, learn it'. She says, 'Politics at its core is a business of numbers. It's how much you can do with an envelope of money. If you are not strong on economics and not numerate, you can't read the budget papers. So, bone up on it because that's where they'll judge you and apply a discount factor.'

She explains that in her era, few women were confident in those areas. 'They might have had the best qualifications in the room, but that wasn't always apparent.' And in the past, women were not typically deployed into portfolios such as defence, national security and treasury. Instead they were pigeon-holed into areas such as social policy portfolios. Being well versed in the economics and numbers 'gives you flexibility. It will make you like every guy in a suit who wants those portfolios, and they do, believe me. It puts you on an even keel and gives you choices'.

(continued)

These are not just words. Peta's approach to continued and forever learning is advice she has lived by throughout her career. In chapter 6, Peta shared with us the story from her first day at school. Reflecting on a lesson learned from that day, Peta recalled, 'You know, that experience has stayed with me. I think, "don't always be the first person to speak. Always let everyone say their piece, but don't be silent either. If you have something to say, speak deliberately."'

In her 16 years in politics, Peta says, 'I had no shame asking questions, I never had any shame asking them, in fact, all my life I've asked questions.'

And when it comes to mistakes, these can be some of the best learning opportunities. Peta says, 'admit it but don't be locked out of the solution. If you are involved in the remedy, you can see the how and why. It's such a good lesson.'

It strikes me that much of Peta's learning has also come from self-awareness, reflection and insight. In life, as in careers, continuous learning is what keeps us adjusted to the forever-changing world, and as the women in this book reveal, the lessons often lie in the mistakes, the moments of doubt and the ability to embrace change.

Finding your voice: ask for a pay rise

In my conversations with the six women and Phil, they all emphasise the importance of having the courage to speak up, and be heard. Of course, knowing this and acting on it are two very different things. One of the most challenging times to do this is when asking for a pay rise or promotion. As I've mentioned, most women I have met would rather resign from a job (even if they love it) than ask for a pay rise or a promotion. The conversation seems to be that hard. Add the feelings of self-doubt and it becomes almost insurmountable. Don't just take it from me though. According to Merrill Lynch and an *Age Wave* report, 61 per cent of women would rather talk about their own death than money.[152]

These are the psychological theories that explain why we do this:

- The loss aversion theory, which in this context means the fear of losing what we have — for example, respect from our boss, or even our job. This makes us avoid the 'risk' of asking.

- We also have what is referred to as 'ego-depletion' (which can play a significant role), whereby the mental energy needed to overcome self-doubt and fear is so overwhelming that people choose the path of least resistance, making them silent.

Although it is important to understand the psychology behind such behaviour, we still need the courage to ask for what we deserve!

Here's how to tackle asking for a pay rise, promotion, extra training and more ... anything that is important to you and requires your strong voice:

1. *Have all facts and information at the ready.*

If it's a pay rise you're after:

- When was your last pay increase?

- Was it above inflation and market?

- Do you receive other benefits such as additional superannuation, health insurance, bonuses and training? All these count towards your total remuneration package.

- Be up to date with knowledge of your industry and job as it provides bargaining power and confidence.

- Compare like with like: job content, education and years of experience; look at job advertisements, recruitment agencies and salary guides.

- Review the job description: are you meeting all requirements? What are the wins?

EARNING POWER

If it's a promotion you're after:

- Are you delivering in your current role?
- What are the job requirements?
- Work out transferable skills.
- For any gaps in skills or capability: be prepared with a solution.
- Highlight what else you bring (soft skills and attributes).
- Consider what you're prepared to do to be successful? What extra time and investment will you commit to? (Use your SWOT analysis!)

If it's upskilling/training you're after:

- What are the costs: how will they translate to a return on investment (ROI)?
- What are the benefits to the business and its customers?

2. *Prepare your mindset.*

- Be calm with a positive outlook.
- Try not to hold onto any dissenting thoughts. Recall positive aspects of your job and employer instead. Positive or negative, these thoughts transfer to your body language and demeanour.
- Part of mindset preparation is viewing your employer's perspective. Seeing the other side is the 101 of smart negotiations.
- Don't do a high pitch as a 'chancer'. It could erode your credibility and integrity and damage relationships, so be mindful.

3. *Practise.*

- How many times in our career do we negotiate a pay rise or ask for a promotion or extra training? Not often. So why do we wing it?

- Practise and say it out loud. Smile and use eye contact. The more you become accustomed to saying the figure and why, the easier it will roll off your tongue.

- When practice is neglected, two outcomes typically occur. At the last minute, you baulk at the figure you had originally psyched yourself up for and ask for less, or your dialogue comes across as blunt and demanding.

- Take notes with you. It is totally okay and expected. It will help you to remain calm and composed.

4. *Have a back-up plan.*

- If you don't get what you set out for, don't default to resigning.

- Find out what needs to be done for you to achieve what you are asking for.

- Ask for a review date. Have this conversation in the current meeting, not later.

- Remain calm and think about the big picture for your whole future.

Even someone as accomplished and self-assured as Nagi from RecipeTin Eats says the first time she negotiated a pay rise, she was 'freaking out'. It's so easy to say, but it's really about finding the courage to do it. The times after that, however, she just thought, 'What's the harm in asking?' And she got it.

Nagi's advice:

Go into the meeting and have a sensible discussion. Don't mention other people's salaries, I really think that undermines the situation. The biggest thing that I would say is to think about what there is to lose. Whatever you are asking for, if you do it professionally, and you're polite about it—whether it's asking for a promotion, or a pay raise, a bonus or more responsibilities, or whatever it is you're asking for—just think What is there to lose? *And if there's nothing to lose, do it in a polite way.*

After all, discussing the salary rise isn't just about money—it's about self-worth and self-advocacy. It's about us wanting others to value our contribution in a way that is fair and deserved. If we can remove these negative emotions and psychological states that tend to work against us during this process, we can focus with confidence on what truly matters.

Every woman's story in this book shows us that we hold the keys to transformation. Only we can redefine our worth, not based on how we are seen, but how we see ourselves. It will take some time, so we must also be patient as we question and rewrite a better narrative, the one we tell others and the one we tell ourselves. It's in the everyday choices we make to push forward, to ask for what we deserve and to support those around us in doing the same.

The wisdom shared throughout this book is more than a collection of powerful and unique voices; it's a lifeline to the future. It's an invitation for all of us to create a world where our daughters inherit not just opportunities but a belief in their boundless potential, and our sons grow up knowing that power is found not in dominance, but in shared strength.

If we take this wisdom to heart, we don't just close the gender pay gap, we create a world where the gap never exists again. This is our moment. It begins with what we choose to do next.

I didn't waste time on barriers that were in my view without justification.

PROFESSOR FIONA WOOD

Conclusion

I FOUGHT A BOY AND WON

I set out to write this book for women. It stemmed from what I saw as 'unfairness' in the workplace and a motivation to inspire women to aim higher and demand more. My resolve grew even stronger when the 'She's Price(d)less' report was released.

The gender pay gap is not just a statistic, it's our lived reality.

Whether viewed through the official data of institutions and organisations such as the WGEA or from my anecdotal evidence, the figures are too similar to ignore: $1 million over a woman's lifetime ... and counting.

When I began this book, my goal was for it to be about *you* and for *you*. But as I sit here writing this final chapter, I can't help but reflect on how much *I* have gained along the way. From meeting and talking with the incredible women featured in this book, I've been given added gifts and treasures of confidence and faith. Dare I say it, I come away with a better view of the world.

The confidence to know it's okay to be forceful, bullish and tough when it's needed. It was liberating to realise I wasn't the only one who navigates the world this way. These words acted as some sort of stamp of, '*You are okay.*'

I am conservative, a rule follower, prudent and respectful of authority ... those older than me, you see where I am going. But I have this other side: a strong and often stubborn streak to seek justice. I cannot stand anything that I see as unfair, or tolerate any form of cruelty or meanness. I step in if I see something that I think is wrong, even if it means bucking the system, going against the flow and disregarding those precious rules I was brought up to follow. Thank you, for sharing with me that sometimes it's okay to be an outlier, change the narrative and seek adventure. *'I thought I was weird.'*

As for 'working your guts out', not thinking of your job as a 'job', thinking that hard work should be a prized attribute, 'getting back up again' and having an 'attitude of knowing anything is possible', what a relief to hear you say the same things. *'I thought there was something wrong with me.'*

As you have been reading *Earning Power*, my hope is that you've gathered small nuggets of advice and insights that show you too are normal and not weird, just an equally special female. We are on the same team.

Thank you to these women for saying yes, females supporting females. A big thank you and a hug to: Julia Ross, Professor Fiona Wood, Nagi Maehashi, Kristina Karlsson, Peta Credlin and Leila McKinnon. I am incredibly grateful for your trust in sharing your messages and stories. Thank you to Phil Kearns for saying yes. Your generous contribution, views and outlook are invaluable. Thank you, ladies and one gent, for the honour and privilege of letting me into that part of your lives.

As a final thought, I'll leave you with this; one of my earliest memories of life's 'unfairness' as a girl.

I fought a boy and won

As a child, due to my dad's job, we travelled a lot. I changed primary schools four times and my brother three times. When you change schools so often, you get accustomed to being the 'new kid' and having to fit in, find your spot, assert yourself and do all you can, not to get picked on. It's a rite of passage as kids.

It's 1979, I was 10 years old, and my brother and I had just settled into grades 3 and 5 respectively at a school in Bendigo, Victoria. Our younger sister was also at the same school, starting in prep.

Coming straight from a beachside school in Western Australia, we joined mid-term, were brown as berries, with white, bleached blonde hair and absolutely no friends. Dropped off each morning by mum, the three of us traipsing through the school gates were painfully conspicuous ... well, at least it felt that way. It's not what you want when you are new and trying all you can to be accepted.

Worse, instead of wearing trainers, like everyone else, Mum made us wear black lace-up school shoes (supposedly better for your feet). They were not cool at all. We were a spectacle and looked like we belonged to a cult. We didn't belong, and it was obvious.

A few weeks in and we are making friends and settling in. Until the boy sitting behind me in class, Andrew, started pulling my pigtails. And he wouldn't stop. Even when we were in the playground, it continued. I was playing hopscotch with my friends and Andrew and his friend John (the most delinquent of Andrew's group) came past. John started to taunt me, calling me names and trying to grab the ends of my hair.

Suddenly, everyone was staring at us, and forming a circle around us. I didn't know what to do. Andrew and John took turns grabbing my hair. I was panicking mildly, so I pushed Andrew to stop him. The circle was tighter now, and all the boys were yelling for him to push me back. 'She's a girl, don't let her do that.'

So, he did. He pushed me and it was on. We were fighting! How did this happen? But I couldn't stop; otherwise I'd get hurt. I was crying but kept fighting back. Then, out of the blue, he got scared, ran away and started climbing up the flagpole, right near the lunch sheds. I was so upset, full of adrenalin and sudden self-righteousness, so I chased him, grabbed his legs and pulled him down to make sure he knew he could never, ever do that to me again.

EARNING POWER

The lunch lady saw us ... I was sent to the principal's office. Mum was called. It hadn't even been one month. Mum was mortified and, when we got home, sharply told me I should never, ever fight. Then she pointed to my brother, Al, and said the same thing. I felt miffed. I was terrified when it was all happening and even cried. But I fought a boy and won. I had a tiny sense of pride but no acknowledgement from Mum. Nothing.

My brother and I discussed it later and agreed Mum was wrong on this one. We needed to defend ourselves at 7 and 10 years. Secretly, we thought Dad felt the same way. From then on, I sneaked my old trainers into my school bag and slipped them on as soon as Mum drove off. Al did the same.

We picked AFL teams to follow — North Melbourne and Carlton — and even adorned the ugly, scratchy, acrylic football jerseys to wear. Anything to fit in.

But, returning to school the next day was not the same. I carried with me a small weight. It wasn't the size 3 Converse sneakers hidden behind my books; it was the realisation that life is different if you are a boy. Mum was right, of course; there is never a place for fighting, but the shock on everyone's face — the principal, other children and my mum — that I fought a boy (and won) stayed with me. I battled my feelings of pride for standing up for myself, with the shame for doing something supposedly a girl should never do.

If I were a boy, there would be no fight. Boys didn't have pigtails then and if they did, they wouldn't have been pulled. There would be no principal or mum called to the principal's office because boys fighting was run of the mill. I saw it happen every lunch time. However, if I were any other girl in that class, there would also not be a fight because ... guess what? They would have accepted the hair pulling.

You might have been smarter than me, knowing it was a battle not easily won. Granted, it's the easier path to take. But, perhaps some battles, even when losing is inevitable, are worth the fight and sometimes these battles are instinctive because we know it's right. That alone counts for something.

Andrew probably remembers that day too, though I suspect his ego has reshaped it, painting a less vivid picture of his defeat. I am sure his buddies and my girlfriends (who did nothing to help, by the way) also remember and it provided a small life lesson for them — at least, I hope it did.

The taunting remained, and it was duly reciprocated, but there was no more pigtail pulling. This was my first serious lesson on who rules the schoolyard, and, later in life, the workplace; the expectations of boys and girls, men and women remain seismically different. I also checked on my brother and sister every lunchtime after that. My sense of duty and responsibility as the older sibling had been established and has stayed with me ever since.

At 10 years old I learned some battles, especially those against injustice, deserve to be fought. Even if we are uncomfortable, even if the world expects us to behave differently, the courage to stand up and speak out can ripple far beyond the moment. I also learned that these small, deeply personal acts of resistance shape our identities and legacies. At that moment, I wasn't just defending myself; I was beginning a lifelong project of questioning the structures that tell us where we belong and what we are worth.

It takes every female to decide what they can do in their life to change it. If every female decides what they're going to do personally to change it, then the world will change rapidly.

JULIA ROSS,
ON GENDER INEQUITY IN
THE WORKPLACE

NOTES

1. Kim BK (2017) *Bias in Babies is a Learned Behavior*, Labroots website, accessed 18 September 2024. https://www.labroots .com/trending/neuroscience/6450/bias-babies-learned-behavior#:~:text=In%20all%20of%20the%20different,to%20 be%20prosocial%2C%20i.e.%20good

2. Kim BK (2017) *Bias in Babies is a Learned Behavior*, Labroots website, accessed 18 September 2024. https://www.labroots .com/trending/neuroscience/6450/bias-babies-learned-behavior#:~:text=In%20all%20of%20the%20different,to%20 be%20prosocial%2C%20i.e.%20good

3. Workplace Gender Equality Agency (WGEA) (2024) *MEDIA RELEASE: New 'Equal Pay Day' campaign says the gender pay gap just doesn't add up*, Australian Government website, accessed 19 September 2024. https://www.wgea.gov.au/newsroom/ New_Equal_Pay_Day_campaign_gpg_just_doesnt_add_ up#:~:text=WGEA%20research%20has%20identified%20 gender,to%20Australia's%20gender%20pay%20gap

4. Wallace BC and Carter RT *Understanding and Dealing With Violence: A Multicultural Approach*, Sage Publications, 2002.

5. Masequesmay G (2021) *Sexism*, Encyclopedia Britannica website, accessed 21 July 2022. https://www.britannica.com/ topic/sexism

6. Statista Research Department (2024) *Share of CEOs of Fortune 500 companies who were women from 1995 to 2020*, Statista website, accessed 18 September 2024. https://www.statista.com/statistics/691192/share-of-women-ceos-fortune-500/#:~:text=U.S.%20share%20of%20female%20CEOs%20in%20Fortune%20500%20companies%201995%2D2020&text=In%201995%2C%20zero%20percent%20of,of%20CEO's%2C%20or%2037%20women

7. Hinchliffe E (2023) *Women CEOs run 10.4% of Fortune 500 companies. A quarter of the 52 leaders became CEO in the last year*, Fortune website, accessed 19 September 2024. https://fortune.com/2023/06/05/fortune-500-companies-2023-women-10-percent

8. Women's Agenda (n.d.) *Women leading ASX 200 companies today*, Women's Agenda website, accessed 19 September 2024. https://womensagenda.com.au/business/women-leading-asx-200-organisations-today

9. Diversity Council Australia Ltd (n.d.) *Capitalising on Culture and Gender in ASX Leadership.* https://www.dca.org.au/wp-content/uploads/2023/06/capitalising_on_culture_and_gender_infographic_final_0.pdf

10. Whiting K (2019) *7 surprising and outrageous stats about gender inequality*, World Economic Forum, accessed 15 October 2024. https://www.weforum.org/agenda/2019/03/surprising-stats-about-gender-inequality

11. Ziv S (2020) *7 Striking Facts About the State of Women in the Workplace*, the muse, accessed 15 October 2024. https://www.themuse.com/advice/7-striking-facts-women-in-the-workplace-2018

12. Whiting K (2019) *7 surprising and outrageous stats about gender inequality*, World Economic Forum, accessed 15 October 2024. https://www.weforum.org/agenda/2019/03/surprising-stats-about-gender-inequality

Notes

13. Pittman T (2016) *1 In 4 Americans Think We'll Colonize Mars Before We See CEO Gender Parity*, Huffpost website, accessed 18 September 2024. https://www.huffpost.com/entry/martians-before-female-ceos_n_573b248de4b060aa78 1b4047

14. OECD Facebook post. https://www.facebook.com/theOECD/posts/women-spend-more-than-25-times-as-much-time-on-unpaid-care-and-domestic-work-tha/ 858273386345104

15. Workplace Gender Equality Agency (WGEA) (2024) *MEDIA RELEASE: New 'Equal Pay Day' campaign says the gender pay gap just doesn't add up*, Australian Government website, accessed 19 September 2024. https://www.wgea .gov.au/newsroom/New_Equal_Pay_Day_campaign_gpg_ just_doesnt_add_up#:~:text=WGEA%20research%20has%20 identified%20gender,to%20Australia's%20gender%20pay%20 gap

16. Murphy B (2024) *These physician specialties have the biggest gender imbalances*, AMA website, accessed 19 September 2024. https://www.ama-assn.org/medical-students/specialty-profiles/these-physician-specialties-have-biggest-gender-imbalances

17. World Bank (2022) *Female labor force participation*, World Bank Group, accessed 23 September 2024. https://genderdata .worldbank.org/en/data-stories/flfp-data-story#:~:text= The%20global%20labor%20force%20participation,do%20 work%2C%20they%20earn%20less

18. Jericho G (2023) *Yes, Australia's gender pay gap is closing. But today's working women will retire before it is fixed*, The Guardian website, accessed 3 October 2024. https://www.theguardian .com/business/grogonomics/2023/jun/22/yes-australias-gender-pay-gap-is-closing-but-todays-working-women-will-retire-before-it-is-fixed

19. Gilchrist K (2024) *Global gender gap could take 134 years to close — but 2024 elections offer hope, WEF says*, CNBC website, accessed 3 October 2024. https://www.cnbc.com/2024/06/11/wef-2024-election-cycle-offers-hope-for-134-year-global-gender-gap.html

20. PM&C Office for Women (2024) *Employment*. https://genderequality.gov.au/sites/default/files/2024-02/Roundtable-Discussion-Paper_Employment.docx

21. World Bank Gender Data Portal (n.d.) *Australia*, World Bank Group website, accessed 19 September 2024. https://genderdata.worldbank.org/en/economies/australia

22. ABS (2021) *Changing female employment over time*, ABS website, accessed 19 September 2024. https://www.abs.gov.au/articles/changing-female-employment-over-time#:~:text=Women's%20participation%20in%20paid%20work,to%20around%2030%25%20in%201966

23. Workplace Gender Equality Agency (WGEA) (2024) *MEDIA RELEASE: New 'Equal Pay Day' campaign says the gender pay gap just doesn't add up*, Australian Government website, accessed 19 September 2024. https://www.wgea.gov.au/newsroom/New_Equal_Pay_Day_campaign_gpg_just_doesnt_add_up#:~:text=WGEA%20research%20has%20identified%20gender,to%20Australia's%20gender%20pay%20gap

24. International Labour Organization (2024) *The gender pay gap*, ILO website, accessed 19 September 2024. https://www.ilo.org/resource/other/gender-pay-gap#:~:text=Gender%20pay%20gaps%20represent%20one,are%20wide%20variations%20across%20countries

25. Economic Development (2022) *Closing gender pay gaps is more important than ever*, United Nations website, accessed 19 September 2024. https://news.un.org/en/story/2022/09/1126901

Notes

26. WGEA (2024) *Publishing employer gender pay gaps FAQ*, Australian Government, accessed 24 September 2024. https://www.wgea.gov.au/about/our-legislation/publishing-employer-gender-pay-gaps#:~:text=Australia's%20national%20gender%20pay%20gap,to%20a%20difference%20of%20%2426%2C400

27. World Economic Forum (2023) *Global Gender Gap Report 2023*, World Economic Forum website, accessed 19 September 2024. https://www.weforum.org/publications/global-gender-gap-report-2023/in-full/benchmarking-gender-gaps-2023/#:~:text=The%20Global%20Gender%20Gap%20score,compared%20to%20last%20year's%20edition

28. Jericho G (2023) *Yes, Australia's gender pay gap is closing. But today's working women will retire before it is fixed*, The Guardian website, accessed 3 October 2024. https://www.theguardian.com/business/grogonomics/2023/jun/22/yes-australias-gender-pay-gap-is-closing-but-todays-working-women-will-retire-before-it-is-fixed

29. Holmes K and Corley D (2016) *The Top 10 Facts About the Gender Wage Gap*, American Progress, accessed 15 October 2024. https://www.americanprogress.org/article/the-top-10-facts-about-the-gender-wage-gap/

30. Perez CC (2021) *Book Review: Invisible Women*, Square, accessed 15 October 2024. https://squaretwo.org/Sq2ArticleHarrisonInvisibleWomen.html

31. Kochhar R (2023) *The Enduring Grip of the Gender Pay Gap*, Pew Research Center website, accessed 19 September 2024. https://www.pewresearch.org/social-trends/2023/03/01/the-enduring-grip-of-the-gender-pay-gap/#:~:text=The%20gender%20pay%20gap%20%E2%80%93%20the,80%20cents%20to%20the%20dollar

32. United Nations (2022) *Closing gender pay gaps is more important than ever*, UN website, accessed 23 September 2024. https://news.un.org/en/story/2022/09/1126901

33. Pathways to Politics for Women (2023) *Global Gender Gap Report 2023*, Pathways to Politics for Women website, accessed 19 September 2024. https://pathwaystopolitics .org.au/knowledge-hub/global-gender-gap-report-2023/#:~:text=At%20the%20current%20rate%20of, spread%20of%20scores%20across%20countries

34. World Economic Forum (2023) *Gender Equality Is Stalling: 131 Years to Close the Gap*, World Economic Forum website, accessed 19 September 2024. https://www.weforum.org/ press/2023/06/gender-equality-is-stalling-131-years-to-close-the-gap/#:~:text=Parity%20has%20advanced%20 by%20only,162%20years%20for%20political%20parity

35. Pew Research Center (2023) *The Enduring Grip of the Gender Pay Gap*, Pew Research Center website, accessed 19 September 2024. https://www.pewresearch.org/social-trends/2023/03/01/the-enduring-grip-of-the-gender-pay-gap/#:~:text=Gender%20pay%20gap%20differs%20 widely%20by%20race%20and%20ethnicity,-Looking%20 across%20racial&text=In%202022%2C%20Black%20 women%20earned,%2C%20making%2093%25%20as%20 much

36. Vrajlal A (2023) *Addressing equal pay needs an intersectional approach*, Missing Perspectives website, accessed 19 September 2024. https://www.missingperspectives.com/posts/ addressing-equal-pay-needs-an-intersectional-approach-cultural-pay-gap

37. RMIT University (2019) *50 years after Australia's historic 'equal pay' decision, the legacy of 'women's work' remains*, RMIT University website, accessed 24 September 2024.

https://www.rmit.edu.au/news/all-news/2019/jun/
equal-pay-anniversary

38. Digital Classroom (n.d.) *Wage equality*, Digital Classroom
website, accessed 19 September 2024. https://digital-
classroom.nma.gov.au/defining-moments/equal-pay-
women#:~:text=In%201969%20the%20Australian%20
Conciliation,to%20provide%20for%20their%20families

39. Karp P (2023) *Women earn $1m less than men over lifetime
and retire with $136,000 less super, study finds*, The Guardian
website, accessed 20 September 2024. https://www
.theguardian.com/australia-news/2023/mar/08/women-
earn-1m-less-than-men-over-lifetime-and-retire-with-
136000-less-super-study-finds

40. WGEA (2022) *Fourth edition of the She's Price(d)less report
released*, Australian Government website, accessed 20
September 2024. https://www.mckinsey.com/au/
our-people/australia-gender-pay-gap-report-2024

41. Jobs and Skills (2024) *Australia Gender in the workforce explored
in labour market panel*, Australian Government website,
accessed 20 September 2024. https://www.jobsandskills
.gov.au/news/gender-workforce-explored-labour-market-
panel#:~:text=Workplace%20Gender%20Equality%20
Agency%20(WGEA,gap%20was%20due%20to%20
discrimination

42. Lim J (2024) *Why Chief Executive Women is calling for
40:40:20 targets*, University of Melbourne website, accessed
20 September 2024. https://mbs.edu/news/Why-Chief-
Executive-Women-is-calling-for-40-40-20-targets

43. WGEA (2023) *Australia's Gender Equality Scorecard*, Australian
Government, accessed 20 September 2024. https://www
.wgea.gov.au/sites/default/files/documents/2022-23 WGEA
Gender Equality Scorecard.pdf

44. Ryan MK and Haslam SA (2005) The glass cliff: Evidence that women are over-represented in precarious leadership positions. *British Journal of management, 16*(2), pp.81–90.

45. UN Women (2024) *Facts and figures: Women's leadership and political participation*, UN Women website, accessed 20 September 2024. https://www.unwomen.org/en/what-we-do/leadership-and-political-participation/facts-and-figures

46. Bowes M (2024) *Woolworths and Virgin Australia CEO exits show 'glass cliff' alive and well*, news.com.au, accessed 3 October 2024. https://www.news.com.au/finance/work/leaders/woolworths-and-virgin-australia-ceo-exits-show-glass-cliff-alive-and-well/news-story/b249a59391d2db378575958e11fa1b8a

47. Sandberg S and Scovell N (2013) *Lean In: Women, Work, and the Will to Lead*, SuperSummary website, accessed 3 October 2024. https://www.supersummary.com/lean-in/important-quotes

48. Women's Bureau (2024) *Median weekly earnings by educational attainment and sex*, US Department of Labor website, accessed 20 September 2024. https://www.dol.gov/agencies/wb/data/earnings/Median-weekly-earnings-educational-sex

49. Kochhar R (2023) *The Enduring Grip of the Gender Pay Gap*, Pew Research Center website, accessed 20 September 2024. https://www.pewresearch.org/social-trends/2023/03/01/the-enduring-grip-of-the-gender-pay-gap/#:~:text=In%20 2022%2C%20women%20with%20at,in%20closing%20 the%20pay%20gap

50. Richter F (2023) *Gender Pay Gap Widens With Education Levels*, Statista website, accessed 20 September 2024. https://www.statista.com/chart/30852/gender-pay-gap-in-the-us-by-education-level

51. Olsen A (2023) *The Gender Agenda 2023: Gender Differences in Australian Higher Education*, SPRE Pty Ltd, accessed 22 November 2024. http://www.spre.com.au/download/SPREGenderAgenda2024.pdf

52. Hare J (2024) *Female graduates beat males on all fronts — except salary*, Financial Review website, accessed 20 September 2024. https://www.afr.com/work-and-careers/education/female-graduates-beat-males-on-all-fronts-except-salary-20240527-p5jh0q

53. QILT (2023) *Graduate Outcomes Survey*, QILT website, accessed 20 September 2024. https://www.qilt.edu.au/surveys/graduate-outcomes-survey-(gos)

54. Change the story (2016) *As Women Take Over a Male-Dominated Field, the Pay Drops*, Change the story website, accessed 3 October 2024. https://changethestoryvt.org/as-women-take-over-a-male-dominated-field-the-pay-drops

55. Miller CC (2016) *As Women Take Over a Male-Dominated Field, the Pay Drops*, The New York Times website, accessed 20 September 2024. https://www.nytimes.com/2016/03/20/upshot/as-women-take-over-a-male-dominated-field-the-pay-drops.html

56. US Bureau of Labor Statistics (2024) *Computer and Information Systems Managers*, US Bureau of Labor Statistics website, accessed 20 September 2024. https://www.bls.gov/ooh/management/computer-and-information-systems-managers.htm#tab-1

57. Miller CC (2016) *As Women Take Over a Male-Dominated Field, the Pay Drops*, The New York Times website, accessed 20 September 2024. https://www.nytimes.com/2016/03/20/upshot/as-women-take-over-a-male-dominated-field-the-pay-drops.html

58. Merrill Lynch (n.d.) *Women and Financial Wellness: Beyond the Bottom Line*, AgeWave website, accessed 20 September 2024. https://www.bls.gov/ooh/management/computer-and-information-systems-managers.htm#tab-1

59. Merrill Lynch (n.d.) *Women and Financial Wellness: Beyond the Bottom Line*, AgeWave website, accessed 20 September 2024. https://www.bls.gov/ooh/management/computer-and-information-systems-managers.htm#tab-1

60. ABS (2024) *Average Weekly Earnings, Australia*, ABS website, accessed 20 September 2024. https://www.abs.gov.au/statistics/labour/earnings-and-working-conditions/average-weekly-earnings-australia/latest-release#cite-window1

61. AIHW (2023) *The health of Australia's females*, Australian Government website, accessed 20 September 2024. https://www.aihw.gov.au/reports/men-women/female-health/contents/who-are

62. Creamer J et al. (2022) *Poverty in the United States: 2021*, United States Census Bureau website, accessed 20 September 2024. https://www.census.gov/library/publications/2022/demo/p60-277.html

63. WHO (2024) *Violence against women*, WHO website, https://www.who.int/news-room/fact-sheets/detail/violence-against-women#:~:text=Estimates%20published%20by%20WHO%20indicate,violence%20is%20intimate%20partner%20violence

64. AIHW (2024) *Family, domestic and sexual violence: Economic and financial impacts*, Australian Government website, accessed 23 September 2024. https://www.aihw.gov.au/family-domestic-and-sexual-violence/responses-and-outcomes/economic-financial-impacts

Notes

65. Burtless G (2016) *The growing life-expectancy gap between rich and poor*, Brookings website, accessed 25 September 2024. https://www.brookings.edu/articles/the-growing-life-expectancy-gap-between-rich-and-poor

66. Burtless G (2016) *The growing life-expectancy gap between rich and poor*, Brookings website, accessed 25 September 2024. https://www.brookings.edu/articles/the-growing-life-expectancy-gap-between-rich-and-poor

67. Goebig M (2022) *Three Beliefs About Confidence That Might Be Holding You Back As A Woman In Business*, Forbes website, accessed 25 September 2024. www.forbes.com/councils/forbescoachescouncil/2022/03/08/three-beliefs-about-confidence-that-might-be-holding-you-back-as-a-woman-in-business

68. Haller S (2018) Gender pay inequality starts at home. parents pay boys twice as much allowance as girls, *USA Today* website, access 05 December 2024. https://www.usatoday.com/story/life/allthemoms/2018/07/03/gender-pay-inequality-parents-allowance-boys-girls/755056002

69. UCL (2023) *Men's overconfidence helps them reach top jobs*, UCL website, accessed 25 September 2024. https://cls.ucl.ac.uk/mens-overconfidence-helps-them-reach-top-jobs

70. Australian Council of Social Service (ACOSS) and UNSW Sydney (2021) *Work, income and health inequity*, accessed 25 September 2024. https://povertyandinequality.acoss.org.au/wp-content/uploads/2021/08/Work-income-and-health-inequity_August-2021.pdf

71. Psychology Today staff (n.d.) *Cognitive Dissonance*, Psychology Today website, accessed 25 September 2024. https://www.psychologytoday.com/us/basics/cognitive-dissonance

72. WGEA (2022) *Fourth edition of the She's Price(d)less report released*, WGEA website, accessed 25 September 2024.

https://www.wgea.gov.au/publications/fourth-edition-of-the-shes-pricedless-report-released

73. WGEA (2024) MEDIA RELEASE: *New 'Equal Pay Day' campaign says the gender pay gap just doesn't add up*, WGEA website, accessed 25 September 2024. https://www.wgea.gov.au/newsroom/New_Equal_Pay_Day_campaign_gpg_just_doesnt_add_up

74. Fotta A (2024) *Gender Wage Gap in the US: Implications for Human Resource Management*, EBSCO website, accessed September 2024. https://openurl.ebsco.com/EPDB%3Agcd%3A2%3A17533698/detailv2?sid=ebsco%3Aplink%3Ascholar&id=ebsco%3Agcd%3A177664948&crl=c

75. Pazzanese C (2020) *Women less inclined to self-promote than men, even for a job*, The Harvard Gazette website, accessed 25 September 2024. https://news.harvard.edu/gazette/story/2020/02/men-better-than-women-at-self-promotion-on-job-leading-to-inequities

76. Goebig M (2022) *Three Beliefs About Confidence That Might Be Holding You Back As A Woman In Business*, Forbes website, accessed 25 September 2024. www.forbes.com/councils/forbescoachescouncil/2022/03/08/three-beliefs-about-confidence-that-might-be-holding-you-back-as-a-woman-in-business

77. Riley Bowles H (2014) *Why Women Don't Negotiate Their Job Offers*, Harvard Business Law website, accessed 25 September 2024. https://hbr.org/2014/06/why-women-dont-negotiate-their-job-offers

78. UCL (2023) *Men's overconfidence helps them reach top jobs*, UCL website, accessed 25 September 2024. https://cls.ucl.ac.uk/mens-overconfidence-helps-them-reach-top-jobs

79. Sure N and Adamecz-Volgyi A (2023) *Analysis: Overconfidence dictates who gets 'top jobs' and research shows men benefit more than*

women, UCL website, accessed 25 September 2024. https://www.ucl.ac.uk/news/2023/apr/analysis-overconfidence-dictates-who-gets-top-jobs-and-research-shows-men-benefit-more

80. American Psychological Association (n.d.) *Resilience*, APA website, accessed 25 September 2024. https://www.apa.org/topics/resilience#:~:text=Resilience%20is%20the%20process%20and,to%20external%20and%20internal%20demands

81. Butler E (2024) *The confidence gap: Why most women have never asked for a pay rise*, Euro News website, accessed 27 September 2024. https://www.euronews.com/business/2024/03/08/the-confidence-gap-why-most-women-have-never-asked-for-a-pay-rise#:~:text=According%20to%20a%20recent%20study,enough%20in%20their%20current%20positions

82. ABS (2024) *Retirement and Retirement Intentions, Australia*, ABS website, accessed 27 September 2024. https://www.abs.gov.au/statistics/labour/employment-and-unemployment/retirement-and-retirement-intentions-australia/latest-release#income-at-retirement

83. ABS (2024) *Average Weekly Earnings, Australia*, ABS website, accessed 27 September 2024. https://www.abs.gov.au/statistics/labour/earnings-and-working-conditions/average-weekly-earnings-australia/latest-release

84. AI Group (2024) *Factsheet: Wage dynamics in Australia*, AI Group website, accessed 27 September 2024. https://www.aigroup.com.au/resourcecentre/research-economics/factsheets/factsheet-wage-dynamics-in-australia/#:~:text=Wages%20growth%20(WPI)&text=Following%20a%20period%20of%20low,run%20average%20of%202.4%25%20p.a

85. Reserve Bank of Australia Inflation Calculator: https://www.rba.gov.au/calculator/annualDecimal.html

86. Chen J (2024) *How to Use the Future Value Formula*, Investopedia website, accessed 27 September 2024. https://www.investopedia.com/terms/f/futurevalue.asp

87. Sammer J (n.d.) *Reward Top Performers Even in Lean Times*, SHRM website, accessed 27 September 2024. https://www.shrm.org/topics-tools/news/hr-magazine/reward-top-performers-even-lean-times

88. Myer R (2023) *Superannuation returns grow as total investments near $3.5 trillion*, The New Daily website, accessed 27 September 2024. https://www.thenewdaily.com.au/finance/superannuation/2023/05/25/superannuation-returns-grow

89. ABS (2005) *Mature age workers*, ABS website, accessed 27 September 2024. https://www.abs.gov.au/Ausstats/abs@.nsf/0/D4CD96E96875500DCA256F7200833041

90. Taylor P, Rolland L and Zhou J (2017) *Retaining Australian older workers – a guide to good practice*, Monash University, accessed 27 September 2024. https://www.monash.edu/__data/assets/pdf_file/0003/2052093/WP2017-02.pdf

91. ABS (2024) *Retirement and Retirement Intentions, Australia*, ABS website, accessed 27 September 2024.

92. Patterson K, Proft, K and Maxwell J (2019) *Older Women's Risk of Homelessness: Background Paper*, Australian Human Rights Commission, accessed 27 September 2024. https://humanrights.gov.au/our-work/age-discrimination/publications/older-womens-risk-homelessness-background-paper-2019

93. BT (2024) *How much super should I aim to have at my age?* BT website, accessed 27 September 2024. https://www.bt.com.au/personal/your-finances/retirement/how-much-super-at-my-age.html#:~:text=there's%20a%20gap%3F-,How%20much%20super%20do%20I%20need%20for%20a%20'comfortable%20retirement,and%20around%20%24595%2C000%20for%20singles

Notes

94. Australian Super (n.d.) *How does your super balance compare?* Australian Super website, accessed 27 September 2024. https://www.australiansuper.com/campaigns/average-balance-planners

95. O'Brien K (2024) *How much do I need to retire in Australia?* The Motley Fool website, accessed 29 September 2024. https://www.fool.com.au/investing-education/how-much-to-retire-australia

96. O'Brien K (2024) *How much do I need to retire in Australia?* The Motley Fool website, accessed 8 October 2024. https://www.fool.com.au/investing-education/how-much-to-retire-australia

97. Mercy Foundation (n.d.) *Older women and homelessness,* Mercy Foundation website, accessed 29 September 2024. https://www.mercyfoundation.com.au/our-focus/ending-homelessness/older-women-and-homelessness/#:~:text=The%202016%20Census%20showed%20that,women%20over%2055%20experiencing%20homelessness

98. Patterson K, Proft K and Maxwell J (2019) *Older Women's Risk of Homelessness: Background Paper,* Australian Human Rights Commission, accessed 27 September 2024. https://humanrights.gov.au/our-work/age-discrimination/publications/older-womens-risk-homelessness-background-paper-2019

99. TWU Super (n.d.) *Not all super payments are the same,* TWU Super website, accessed 8 October 2024. https://www.twusuper.com.au/employer-super/how-to-calculate-super/reportable-super-contributions/#:~:text=What%20are%20reportable%20employer%20super,12%25%20on%201%20July%202025

100. Zenger J (2021) *The Confidence Gap In Men And Women: How To Overcome It,* Zenger Folkman website, accessed

29 September 2024. https://zengerfolkman.com/articles/
the-confidence-gap-in-men-and-women-how-to-
overcome-it/#:~:text=Considering%20the%20confidence
%20gap%2C%20gender,differ%20in%20quality%20or%20
quantity

101. UC Davis Advance (n.d.) *Women Don't Ask: Negotiation and the Gender Divide*, UC Davis Advance website. https://ucd-advance.ucdavis.edu/post/women-dont-ask-negotiation-and-gender-divide#:~:text=Women%20 Suffer%20When%20They%20Don,to%20negotiate%20 a%20first%20salary

102. Plath, S (1971) *The Bell Jar*, Faber and Faber.

103. Plath, S (1971) *The Bell Jar*, Faber and Faber, page 62.

104. Festinger L (1954) *A Theory of Social Comparison Processes*, Sage Journals website, accessed 3 October 2024. https:// journals.sagepub.com/doi/10.1177/001872675400700202

105. Kayala H, Madhu P and Werkun E (2023) *Social Comparison on Social Media*, OxJournal website, accessed 3 October 2024. https://www.oxjournal.org/social-comparison-on-social-media

106. Walsh D (2022) *Study: Social media use linked to decline in mental health*, MIT Sloan School of Management website, accessed 3 October 2024. https://mitsloan.mit.edu/ideas-made-to-matter/study-social-media-use-linked-to-decline-mental-health

107. World Food Program USA (2021) *Women Do 2.6 Times More Domestic Work Than Men. Here's a Look Inside 10 of Their Kitchens*, World Food Program USA website, accessed 3 October 2024. https://www.wfpusa.org/articles/kitchens-in-crisis-how-mothers-prepare-meals-in-times-of-extreme-conflict/#:~:text=Imagine%20cooking%20a%20meal%20 without,feed%20themselves%20and%20their%20families

Notes

108. Sumra MK and Schillaci MA (2015) *Stress and the Multiple-Role Woman: Taking a Closer Look at the 'Superwoman'*, National Library of Medicine website, accessed 3 October 2024. https://www.ncbi.nlm.nih.gov/pmc/articles/PMC4376732

109. Sumra MK and Schillaci MA (2015) *Stress and the Multiple-Role Woman: Taking a Closer Look at the 'Superwoman'*, National Library of Medicine website, accessed 3 October 2024. https://www.ncbi.nlm.nih.gov/pmc/articles/PMC4376732

110. McKinsey & Company (2024) *Readying for a recession?* McKinsey & Company website, accessed 4 October 2024. https://www.mckinsey.com/featured-insights/sustainable-inclusive-growth/charts/readying-for-a-recession

111. Waugh B (2014) *Dads Who Share the Load Bolster Daughters' Aspirations*, APS website, accessed 3 October 2024. https://www.psychologicalscience.org/news/releases/dads-who-share-the-load-bolster-daughters-aspirations.html#:~:text=Fathers%20who%20help%20with%20household,the%20Association%20for%20Psychological%20Science.

112. Science Daily (2014) *Dads who do chores bolster daughters' aspirations*, Science Daily website, accessed 3 October 2024. https://www.sciencedaily.com/releases/2014/05/140528105254.htm

113. Hunt V et al. (2018) *Delivering through Diversity*, McKinsey & Company, accessed 10 October 2024. https://www.mckinsey.com/~/media/mckinsey/business functions/organization/our insights/delivering through diversity/delivering-through-diversity_full-report.pdf

114. Science Daily (2014) *Dads who do chores bolster daughters' aspirations*, Science Daily website, accessed 3 October

2024. https://www.sciencedaily.com/releases/2014/05/140528105254.htm

115. Science Daily (2014) *Dads who do chores bolster daughters' aspirations*, Science Daily website, accessed 3 October 2024. https://www.sciencedaily.com/releases/2014/05/140528105254.htm

116. Ton That C (2014) *Dads who do household chores more likely to have ambitious daughters: study*, CTV News website, accessed 3 October 2024. https://www.ctvnews.ca/health/dads-who-do-household-chores-more-likely-to-have-ambitious-daughters-study-1.1842286#:~:text=%E2%80%9CThis%20suggests%20girls%20grow%20up,play%20a%20unique%20gatekeeper%20role.%E2%80%9D

117. Ton That C (2014) *Dads who do household chores more likely to have ambitious daughters: study*, CTV News website, accessed 3 October 2024. https://www.ctvnews.ca/health/dads-who-do-household-chores-more-likely-to-have-ambitious-daughters-study-1.1842286#:~:text=%E2%80%9CThis%20suggests%20girls%20grow%20up,play%20a%20unique%20gatekeeper%20role.%E2%80%9D

118. OECD (n.d.) *Gender equality and work*, OECD website, accessed 3 October 2024. https://www.oecd.org/en/topics/sub-issues/gender-equality-and-work.html

119. AIFS (2018) *Stay-at-home fathers in Australia*, AIFS website, accessed 3 October 2024. https://aifs.gov.au/research/research-reports/stay-home-fathers-australia#:~:text=Overall%2C%20these%20analyses%20find%20that,up%20from%2068%2C500%20in%202011

120. Slobojan I (2023) *The Impact of Masculinity and Gender Norms on Men's Mental Health in the U.S.: A Literature Review*, Portland State University, accessed 5 October 2024. https:/pdxscholar.library.pdx.edu/cgi/viewcontent.cgi?article=2638&context=honorstheses#:~:text=All%20

of%20the%20facets%20tie,wellbeing%20and%20help%20
seeking%20behavior

121. VicHealth (2022) *Understanding masculinities and Health: How social norms impact wellbeing*, VicHealth website, accessed 4 October 2024. https://www.vichealth.vic.gov.au/news-publications/research-publications/masculinities-and-health

122. Australian Unions (n.d.) *Paternity Leave and Partner Leave*, Australian Unions website, accessed 4 October 2024. https://www.australianunions.org.au/factsheet/paternity-leave

123. Smith F (2016) *This is why men don't go home to look after the baby*, ANZ bluenotes website, accessed 4 October 2024. https://www.anz.com.au/bluenotes/2016/05/this-is-why-men-don-t-go-home-to-look-after-the-baby

124. Petrie C (2021) *Meet the 'latte pappas': Stay-at-home dads in Sweden*, The Press and Journal website, accessed 4 October 2024. https://www.pressandjournal.co.uk/fp/education/3729300/paternity-leave-sweden-latte-pappas

125. Nordic Council of Ministers (2019) *Shared and paid parental leave*, accessed 5 October 2024. https:/norden.diva-portal.org/smash/get/diva2:1240186/FULLTEXT03.pdf

126. Tsusaka M, Reeves M, Hurder S and Harnoss J (2017) *Diversity at Work*, BCG website, accessed 4 October 2024. https://www.bcg.com/publications/2017/diversity-at-work

127. Tsusaka M, Reeves M, Hurder S and Harnoss J (2017) *Diversity at Work*, BCG website, accessed 4 October 2024. https://www.bcg.com/publications/2017/diversity-at-work

128. Juneja V (2024) *Engaging Men as Allies*, HRO Today website, accessed 4 October 2024. https://www.hrotoday.com/diversity-inclusion/engaging-men-as-allies/#:~:text=Worldwide%20research%20by%20BCG%20shows,where%20men%20are%20not%20involved

129. McKinsey & Company (2024) *Readying for a recession?* McKinsey & Company website, accessed 4 October 2024. https://www.mckinsey.com/featured-insights/sustainable-inclusive-growth/charts/readying-for-a-recession

130. McKinsey & Company (2024) *Readying for a recession?* McKinsey & Company website, accessed 4 October 2024. https://www.mckinsey.com/featured-insights/sustainable-inclusive-growth/charts/readying-for-a-recession

131. McKinsey & Company (2024) *Readying for a recession?* McKinsey & Company website, accessed 4 October 2024. https://www.mckinsey.com/featured-insights/sustainable-inclusive-growth/charts/readying-for-a-recession

132. Law Council of Australia (2018) *Sexual harassment in the workplace*, Law Council of Australia website, accessed 4 October 2024. https://lawcouncil.au/policy-agenda/advancing-the-profession/equal-opportunities-in-the-law/sexual-harassment-in-the-workplace#:~:text=Sexual%20harassment%20is%20unwanted%20or,participating%20in%20the%20legal%20profession

133. Law Council of Australia (2018) *Sexual harassment in the workplace*, Law Council of Australia website, accessed 4 October 2024. https://lawcouncil.au/policy-agenda/advancing-the-profession/equal-opportunities-in-the-law/sexual-harassment-in-the-workplace#:~:text=Sexual%20harassment%20is%20unwanted%20or,participating%20in%20the%20legal%20profession

134. Australian Government (2024) *Status of Women Report Card 2024*, Australian Government website, accessed 4 October 2024. https://genderequality.gov.au/status-women-report-cards/2024-report-card

135. Australian Government (2024) *Status of Women Report Card 2024*, Australian Government website, accessed 4 October 2024.

https://genderequality.gov.au/status-women-report-cards/2024-report-card

136. ANROWS (2024) *One in seven Australian adults report engaging in workplace technology-facilitated sexual harassment new study finds*, ANROWS website, accessed 4 October 2024. https://www.anrows.org.au/media-releases/one-in-seven-australian-adults-report-engaging-in-workplace-technology-facilitated-sexual-harassment-new-study-finds

137. Long C (2024) *One in seven people admit to using tech to sexually harass colleagues at work, new data shows*, ABC News website, accessed 4 October 2024. https://www.abc.net.au/news/2024-04-30/sexual-harassment-australia-government-women/103782376

138. AHRC (2018) *Industries where sexual harassment occurs*, infographic, accessed 4 October 2024. https://humanrights.gov.au/sites/default/files/infographics_ahrc_workplace_sh_2018.pdf

139. Hewlett SA (2013) *Mentors Are Good. Sponsors Are Better*, The New York Times website, accessed 4 October 2024. https://www.nytimes.com/2013/04/14/jobs/sponsors-seen-as-crucial-for-womens-career-advancement.html

140. Juneja V (2024) *Engaging Men as Allies*, HRO Today website, accessed 4 October 2024. https://www.hrotoday.com/diversity-inclusion/engaging-men-as-allies/#:~:text=Worldwide%20research%20by%20BCG%20shows,where%20men%20are%20not%20involved

141. Baxter J et al. (2023) *Gender Gaps in Unpaid Domestic and Care Work: Putting The Pandemic in (a Life Course) Perspective*, Wiley Online Library, accessed 14 October 2024. https://onlinelibrary.wiley.com/doi/full/10.1111/1467-8462.12538#aere12538-bib-0002

142. Free Network (n.d.) *Global Gender Gap in Unpaid Care: Why Domestic Work Still Remains a Woman's Burden*, Free Network

website, accessed 6 October 2024. https://freepolicybriefs
.org/2021/12/20/gender-gap-unpaid-care

143. Free Network (n.d.) *Global Gender Gap in Unpaid Care: Why Domestic Work Still Remains a Woman's Burden*, Free Network website, accessed 6 October 2024. https://freepolicybriefs .org/2021/12/20/gender-gap-unpaid-care

144. Everding, G (2014) *Spouse's personality influences career success, study finds*, Washington University website, accessed 6 October 2024. https://source.washu.edu/2014/09/ spouses-personality-influences-career-success-study-finds/

145. WGEA (2022) *Fourth edition of the She's Price(d)less report released*, Australian Government website, accessed 6 October 2024. https://www.wgea.gov.au/publications/ fourth-edition-of-the-shes-pricedless-report-released

146. Everding, G (2014) *Spouse's personality influences career success, study finds*, Washington University website, accessed 6 October 2024. https://source.washu.edu/2014/09/ spouses-personality-influences-career-success-study-finds/

147. Hopcroft, RL (2023) *Husbands with Much Higher Incomes Than Their Wives Have a Lower Chance of Divorce*, Institute for Family Studies website, accessed 6 October 2024. https:// ifstudies.org/blog/husbands-with-much-higher- incomes-than-their-wives-have-a-lower-chance-of-divorce- #:~:text=For%20the%20more%20recent%20 marriage,husband's%20income%20was%20more%20than

148. Chicago Booth (2103) *When Women Earn More Than Their Husbands*, Chicago Booth website, accessed 6 October 2024. https://www.chicagobooth.edu/media-relations-and- communications/press-releases/when-women-earn-more- than-their-husbands

149. Vohs KD (2015) *Money Priming Can Change People's Thoughts, Feelings, Motivations, and Behaviors: An Update on*

10 Years of Experiments, accessed 6 October 2024. https://carlsonschool.umn.edu/sites/carlsonschool.umn.edu/files/2019-04/vohs_2015_money_priming_review_replications_jepg.pdf

150. Zubair, M (2023) *Why is it important to have female mentors at work?* Together website, accessed 6 October 2024. https://www.togetherplatform.com/blog/female-mentors#:~:text=According%20to%20a%20global%20study,never%20had%20a%20formal%20mentor

151. Lin G et al. (2021) *The impact of gender in mentor–mentee success: Results from the Women's Dermatologic Society Mentorship Survey*, National Library of Medicine website, accessed 6 October 2024. https://www.ncbi.nlm.nih.gov/pmc/articles/PMC8484982

152. The Motley Fool (2018) *61% of Women Would Rather Talk About Their Own Death Than Money*, Nasdaq website, accessed 6 October 2024. https://www.nasdaq.com/articles/61-women-would-rather-talk-about-their-own-death-money-2018-05-22